DEPARTMENT OF EDUCATION AND SCIENCE

REPORT OF THE COMMITTEE OF INQUIRY INTO THE TEACHING OF ENGLISH LANGUAGE

APPOINTED BY THE SECRETARY OF STATE
UNDER THE CHAIRMANSHIP OF
SIR JOHN KINGMAN, FRS

MARCH 1988

London: Her Majesty's Stationery Office

Committee of Inquiry into the Teaching of English Language

Chairman: Sir John Kingman FRS
Secretary: P Gannon HMI

Elizabeth House York Road London SE1 7PH
Room 6/23

Direct Line   01-934 9437
Switchboard 01-934 9000
GTN Number 2914

Telex 23171

Your reference

Our reference

17th March, 1988

Dear Secretary of State,

I have the honour to submit the report of the Committee on the Teaching of English Language.

It must be a primary objective of the educational system to enable and encourage every child to use the English language to the fullest effect in speaking, writing, listening and reading. It is arguable that such mastery can be achieved without an explicit knowledge of the structure of the language, but there is no positive advantage in such ignorance. And the worst reason for avoiding teaching about language is that teachers are not confident in their own knowledge.

We argue that it is possible to give a sound and accessible description of the structure and uses of the English language, and that all teachers should have an appropriate familiarity with that description. They will then be able to use their professional judgement about the extent to which that description should be made explicit to their pupils at different stages of their education.

We believe that the proper preparation of teachers is central to the questions you asked us to examine. Our recommendations carry serious implications for both initial and in-service training, and we urge you to act on them without delay.

The issues within our terms of reference deserve continuing study and debate, and some of them will no doubt be taken up by the working party on the English curriculum which will succeed us. We hope that we have laid a useful foundation.

Yours sincerely,

John Kingman

The Right Honourable Kenneth Baker, MP,
Secretary of State for Education and Science

Acknowledgement

The work of the Committee would have been impossible without the support of our Secretariat, and notably of Mr Peter Gannon, HMI, Secretary to the Committee, and Mrs Rosemary Hussain, DES, Assistant Secretary to the Committee. To them we express our gratitude for help which went far beyond the call of duty, and which enabled the Committee to do justice to a mass of complex evidence and to produce a report within a very tight deadline.

Contents

Chapter *1* *Setting the scene*

1.

... the danger confronting English today is not so much indifference as distraction.

Those words, from the Newbolt Report of 1921, strike a chord nearly 70 years later. The Newbolt Committee was discussing the risk that much of English as a distinctive subject might be crowded out of the school curriculum by the demands of other ways of developing children's abilities, aptitudes and experience to meet the needs of adult life.

2.   There is little fear today that English might vanish from the school timetable or scheme of work. But there is a widespread concern that pressures on time and energy, together with inadequacies in the professional education and training of teachers and a misunderstanding of the nature of children's learning, are causing important areas of English language teaching to be neglected, to the detriment of children's facility with words. As in 1921, indifference is not the problem: teachers are anxious to develop children's capacity to use language effectively. The distraction today is in part the belief that this capacity can and should be fostered only by exposure to varieties of English language; that conscious knowledge of the structure and working of the language is unnecessary for effective use of it; that attempting to teach such knowledge induces boredom, damages creativity and may yet be unsuccessful; and that the enterprise entails imposing an authoritarian view of a standard language which will be unacceptable to many communities in our society.

Our task   3.   Our task required us to probe these assumptions. We were appointed by the Secretary of State for Education and Science at the beginning of 1987 to recommend a model of the English language as a basis for teacher training and professional discussion, and to consider how far and in what ways that model should be made explicit to pupils at various stages of education. The Committee's full terms of reference and membership are given in Appendices 1 and 2.

4.   We have been grateful for written and oral evidence from 239 individuals and organisations within and outside the educational and academic worlds. Appendix 4 catalogues the sources of evidence. We have also visited a sample of 14 primary and 16 secondary schools, and six teacher training institutions. The Committee wishes to record its gratitude to all those sources. The institutions visited were both co-operative and illuminating: the written evidence was clearly the result of extensive and concentrated thought. Attention has been paid, throughout the report, to that mass of informing, if unattributed evidence. Our membership has included a wide variety of backgrounds: primary and secondary schooling, local authority services, higher education and teacher training, academic language and literature studies, writing, journalism, broadcasting and industry. Our deliberations have been extensively informed both by professional advice on what is realistic and

possible for the education service to do, and by the expectations of pupils, parents, employers and the general public.

5.   The problem is not a new one. Nor has there been a lack of attempts to tackle it. We owe a particular debt to the Bullock Committee. In March 1975, the Committee of Inquiry appointed by the Secretary of State for Education and Science under the chairmanship of Sir Alan Bullock published its report. It has had great influence on the teaching and learning of English in British schools. In the 609 pages of that report, which included 333 recommendations, one of the most important themes was the competence of both teachers and pupils in respect of their knowledge of and about the English language. The Bullock Report valuably drew attention to the issue and made significant recommendations about teacher training needs. Most teachers agree that many of these recommendations have not been implemented and that their implications have not been followed through with sufficient rigour or in detail.

6.   Other factors influenced the course of debate. The surveys of primary and secondary education by Her Majesty's Inspectorate in the late 1970s drew attention to a number of observable deficiencies in the use of language by a significant proportion of pupils. There were some disturbing features of provision in many schools: unduly low expectations of pupils' capabilities; a narrow diet of writing and reading taught separately and in isolation from practical contexts; too much emphasis on restricted mechanical tasks at the expense of the wide range of writing needed in adult life; not enough attention to extending the variety and depth of children's reading and their enthusiasm for it; and little effort put into encouraging critical thinking. Yet the examples of what could be achieved in schools where the language work was strong showed that the picture need not be bleak.

7.   Similar evidence from other areas of the curriculum led to a growing belief that the problem lay in the patchiness of provision. Greater consistency was essential, in what was offered and in how it was organised and delivered, so that the practice of the majority more closely approached that of the best. In this way all children would receive their proper educational entitlement. It was also essential for the rising generation to be adequately equipped to meet the demands of contemporary society and the competitive economy nationally and internationally. This concern, articulated notably in 1976 by the then Prime Minister, Mr James Callaghan, in a speech at Ruskin College, Oxford, resulted in a series of initiatives by the Government to focus attention on the quality and coherence of the curriculum. An important milestone was the 1984 White Paper, *Better Schools*, presented by the then Secretary of State, Sir Keith Joseph.

'English from 5 to 16'   8.   One product of this development was the series of Curriculum Matters discussion documents by H M Inspectorate. The first of these publications, *English from 5 to 16*, proposed four aims for English teachers. After dealing with the first three – involving speech, reading and writing – the paper described the fourth aim as:

to teach pupils *about* language, so that they achieve a working knowledge of its structure and of the variety of ways in which meaning is made, so that they have a vocabulary for discussing it, so that they can use it with greater awareness, and because it is interesting.

9. Widespread objection was raised against that fourth aim, although there was support for it in some quarters. The Inspectorate's follow-up publication (*English from 5 to 16: The Responses to Curriculum Matters 1*) reported that they had accordingly asked those who had commented what they judged teachers should be expected to know about language and about language development in children.

Some noted that a substantial in-service programme would be needed to prepare teachers to handle the listed objectives . . . As for what should be taught, either to teachers or pupils, while there were a few individually helpful contributions, there were no clear trends except for the widespread and vigorous rejection of grammatical analysis . . . There is also a clear need and some growing willingness to settle an agenda and ultimately a curriculum for this aim, but it is also plain that it will be a long time before the professional unity required to implement a policy can be arrived at. The growth of a stronger accord might be assisted by an enquiry to focus attention on the matter, with the ultimate object of drawing up recommendations as to what might be taught to intending teachers, to those in post and to pupils in schools.

The national curriculum

10. It was largely in response to that recommendation that the Secretary of State appointed our Committee. We have been clear from the outset, however, that it was not our task merely to revisit the territory traversed so thoroughly by the Bullock Committee. Such an endeavour would be pointless, 12 years later and in much changed circumstances. Indeed, in the early stages of our work, the Secretary of State announced his proposals for the establishment of a national curriculum. These, now embodied in the Education Reform Bill currently before Parliament, place English as one of the core subjects, with programmes of study, attainment targets and related assessment arrangements to be statutorily prescribed for each of the key educational stages between the ages of 5 and 16. The Secretary of State's working group on English which is to be set up to advise on the contents of these prescribed elements, as a basis for consultation before they are given statutory effect, will for part of its deliberations be relying on our Committee's recommendations as to the knowledge pupils need about language. Our respective terms of reference will have that much in common. Yet it is not our responsibility, but that of the working group, to survey the whole field of English, including literature and drama. We touch on these broader aspects only as much as is necessary to illustrate the significance of our model of the structure and workings of language for the cultivation of more effective communication and understanding of what is spoken and written.

11. Nor do we see it as part of our task to plead for a return to old-fashioned grammar teaching and learning by rote. We have been impressed by the evidence we have received that this gave an inadequate account of the English language by treating it virtually as a branch of Latin, and constructing a rigid prescriptive code rather than a dynamic description of language in use. It was also ineffective as a means of developing a command of English in all its manifestations. Equally, at the other extreme, we reject the belief that any notion of correct or incorrect use of language is an affront to personal liberty. We also reject the belief that knowing how to use terminology in which to speak of language is undesirable. Language is, as a matter of observable fact, plainly governed by a series of conventions related to the varying audiences, contexts and purposes of its use. Successful communication depends upon a recognition and accurate use of the rules and conventions. Command of these rules and conventions is more likely to increase the freedom of the individual than diminish it.

Our starting-point

12.   We take it as axiomatic that a primary objective of the educational system must be to enable and encourage every child to use the English language to the fullest effect in speaking, writing, listening and reading. We set out the rationale for this starting-point in **Chapter 2** of this report. It is arguable that such mastery might be achieved without explicit knowledge of the structure of the language or the ways it is used in society. But there is no positive advantage in such ignorance. It is just as important to teach about our language environment as about our physical environment, or about the structure of English as about the structure of the atom. And since we believe that knowledge about language, made explicit at that moment when the pupil is ready, can underpin and promote mastery as well, the argument is even stronger.

A model of the English language

13.   We have tackled this objective by constructing, as our terms of reference invite us to do, a model of the English language. In this context, 'model' does not, of course, mean an exemplar that is to be copied, but rather a representation that is appropriate to the purpose in hand, in this case 'a model that will serve as the basis of how teachers are trained to understand how the English language works and inform professional discussion on all aspects of English teaching'.

14.   In the school curriculum English is unique: the child begins to acquire language before school, without it no other processes of thought and study can take place, and it continues to be central throughout life. These facts reinforce the desirability, which was frequently expressed in the evidence and which we accept, of a model of *language in use*. Consequently, we have constructed a model which takes account of the uses of language as well as its forms and techniques.

15.   We have recognised the concerns, expressed in much of the evidence, that a detailed and prescriptive model could constrain the scope of the experiences of language to which pupils would be exposed, and the freedom to experiment and to adapt teaching to the needs of particular classes and individuals. This freedom is, in our opinion, essential for the practice and development of the teaching of English.

16.   Yet while we are convinced that there must be scope for some variety in patterns in the teaching of English, we have equally no doubt that, since all pupils are entitled to an education which will equip them to use the English language to the best of their abilities, all teachers of English need some explicit knowledge of the forms and the uses of the English language. We have constructed our model to indicate what this knowledge should encompass.

17.   The model is presented in **Chapter 3**. For the reasons already given, it is set out in broad outline and not in detail. It is supplemented by the list of publications in Appendix 7. They offer a variety of content and treatment, from which teachers and teacher trainers can choose aspects of the model that are appropriate for their needs. The list is by no means exhaustive. Books that some might find especially useful may well have been omitted, and good new books will undoubtedly appear.

Using the model

18.   In **Chapter 4** we illustrate some typical ways in which the model can be used in the classroom. **Chapter 5** offers the Committee's view of the educational entitlement of children, in terms of their knowledge about language; and proposes some targets for the knowledge, skills and understanding they might be expected to display at various educational

stages, together with the implications for the assessment of these. **Chapter 6** deals with teachers' professional education and training. It is followed by a summary of our recommendations, and by appendices covering the Committee's terms of reference and membership, evidence, a glossary, and a bibliography.

19.   The Committee's threefold terms of reference are fulfilled in the core of the report. First, we were asked to recommend a model: it is set out in Chapter 3. Secondly, the principles which should guide teachers on how far and in what ways the model should be made explicit to pupils are embodied in Chapter 4. Finally, the attainment targets for pupils are presented in Chapter 5. To gain a clear picture of the relationships between these strands and the rationale for our proposals, however, the report should be read as a whole.

Chapter  The importance of knowledge about language

Introduction: Language in adult life

1. In language lies the most important difference between mankind and the rest of the animal kingdom. Language expresses identity, enables co-operation, and confers freedom. In language we create a symbolic model of the world, in which past and present are carried forward to the future. Language is the naming of experience, and what we name we have power over.

2. People need expertise in language to be able to participate effectively in a democracy. There is no point in having access to information that you cannot understand, or having the opportunity to propose policies which you cannot formulate. People receive information and misinformation in varying proportions from, among others, family and friends, work mates, advertisers, journalists, priests, politicians and pressure groups. A democratic society needs people who have the linguistic abilities which will enable them to discuss, evaluate and make sense of what they are told, as well as to take effective action on the basis of their understanding. The working of a democracy depends on the discriminating use of language on the part of all its people. Otherwise there can be no genuine participation, but only the imposition of the ideas of those who are linguistically capable. As individuals, as well as members of constituencies, people need the resources of language both to defend their rights and to fulfil their obligations.

3. Effective use of language, and an understanding of its principles, will ease the way in those humdrum passages of life where tax returns, mortgage agreements, insurance claims are to be completed; where manuals for the installation of washing-machines are to be understood; where meaning has to be disentangled from a leaflet whose message may be important but whose expression is obscure. In what might be called the carpentry of life, language should be the sharpest instrument.

4. Its edge is sometimes blunted in places of work, where, as evidence presented to the Committee suggests, actual performance is impaired by letters or reports expressed in English that is sometimes incomprehensible, or instructions where misuse of words and emphasis creates misunderstanding. Competence in language is essential to competence in any job.

5. But the practical uses of clear and simple communication are sufficiently obvious. A more complex consideration is the function of language in identifying the individual in relation to the society, and societies, to which he or she belongs. The dialect usages of family and immediate circle are sufficient to their purposes; but membership of the smaller group entails membership of the larger, and for the wider community – that of the nation and the world – the standard language will be indispensable. Of course, in acquiring the standard language, we do not abandon the variation – each has its own authenticity, and to move with facility between them is to develop a versatility in language, a linguistic repertoire, which should be open to all.

6.   We live in times in which social and technological change is taking place at an unprecedented rate and we face an unknowable future. It may be difficult to suggest what bearing this predicament should have on the school curriculum, but to try to develop adaptability must be a sound strategy. Ability in language can contribute powerfully to adaptability, as a resource for continued education, for the acquisition of new knowledge and skills and for widening the accessible range of jobs.

7.   Round the city of Caxton, the electronic suburbs are rising. To the language of books is added the language of television and radio, the elliptical demotic of the telephone, the processed codes of the computer. As the shapes of literacy multiply, so our dependence on language increases. But if language motivates change, it is itself changed. To understand the principles on which that change takes place should be denied to no one.

Language and the child

8.   If language plays such an important part in the lives of adult human beings, then it must also play a very large part in the development of pupils in schools. That is generally acknowledged in the central aims of English as a school subject, which – whatever other functions it may have – is present in the curriculum to enable pupils to emerge from school able to read, write, talk and listen competently. By 'competently' we mean able to cope with the linguistic demands of adult life as outlined in the foregoing section. The skills, perceptions and knowledge that we are advocating will be of value to all pupils, and should in no way be the exclusive privilege of the more able.

9.   English teachers are inevitably concerned with pupils' intellectual, social, personal and aesthetic development. We therefore consider these four aspects of children's growth and comment on the importance of language to each – bearing in mind that each must be considered in relation to the others.

Language in relation to intellectual development

10.   Language is the instrument of intellectual development: it permits children to go beyond their own limited experience and to encounter the thoughts, hypotheses, explanations and analyses of the greatest human minds. The Bullock Report deals with the relations between language and thought persuasively and at some length in its Chapter 4. The child should never be limited to reading or hearing only that which is embedded in everyday experience. Language can create for the child hitherto undreamed-of domains. A partially understood word may pull the child into awareness of a concept never before encountered; a partially understood expression act as a signpost to thoughts as yet unformed. This is one reason why it is so important that children should read literature which stimulates and makes new demands, both linguistic and emotional, upon the reader.

11.

Learning to direct one's own mental processes with the aid of words or signs is an integral part of the process of concept formation. (Vygotsky)

The acquisition of new and difficult concepts, which is integral to education in any subject, is dependent above all upon language. So it becomes most important to lead children beyond their everyday experience, by all possible pedagogic means, to widen and refine their vocabularies, to help them make maximum use of their command of language and to help them extend that command. It we are to help pupils function intellectually – and we take this to be a prime purpose of education – we must spend time in English classes examining words and how each contributes to the meaning of a sentence. We need to put pupils into situations where they are bound to reflect upon the complex associations of words themselves and to value words not just as currency – the small change passed between individuals in order to communicate easily – but as powerful aids to thinking.

12.   There is a vast literature dealing with how children acquire language in the process of cognitive development. From this, we know that the child's early experience of language is, as we have seen, embedded in the context in which the language occurs. In the first months of speaking, children will learn words and simple grammatical structures which will enable them to talk about things which are contextually immediate in the situation of speech, what is happening at the time of speaking, or what can be made to happen in the here and now. Gradually, however, they learn, with increasing sophistication, to speak of things independently of context, things which are no longer actually in view, and of events that have happened in the past or might happen in the future.

13.   By an incremental growth of language, used and encountered in increasingly complex networks of meanings, children are enabled to perceive patterns in their experience, to give an account (if only to themselves) of the world as they perceive it and to recognise other, perhaps conflicting accounts. Increasing control of otherwise undifferentiated experience is thereby achieved, so leading children towards the linguistic capacities of adulthood with which we began.

Language in relation to social development

14.   Children normally belong to at least three social groups – the family, the peer group and the wider group, in social terms, of their 'public' world. The public world of children is largely bounded by the school, where Standard English will be the norm. In each of these groups, the conventions of language behaviour are likely to be different and children ought, in our view, to be aware of how all three have their own legitimacy. These conventions may be associated with different accents, different dialects and (in the case of some communities) different languages.

15.   Very often these conventions are felt to be in conflict. They also overlap – 'street' and 'home' language perhaps more so with one another than with school language. A Yorkshire child may say *nowt* and *summat* both among friends and in the family, but may switch to *nothing* and *something* in the classroom. Conversely, street expressions which a child may have learned it is unwise to use in the home may well turn up in school work under the sanctuary afforded by the need for realistic dialogue in stories. Again, a child might dilute or bowdlerise street expressions for home consumption, editing them even more drastically for school use. Thus, directly their horizons begin to expand beyond the immediate family, children make judgements about language and the way they must adapt their speech to fit into patterns accepted by particular social groups. Such patterns vary at different levels of linguistic complexity. The instance of *nowt* as distinct from *nothing* is at the level of word choice. Variations can occur at other levels. For example, it is regular in West Indian speech to say *he go* rather than *he goes*, just as some regional English usages dictate *he do* rather than *he does*. So parts of words may vary in a regular fashion, as may syntactic choices, as well as accent or idiomatic expressions.

16.   The child needs to operate effectively in home, street and school language. Ultimately these three 'languages' (though by now they will be far less compartmentalised) will evolve into home or work language and the various sub-divisions of that more or less formal language which is used in books, and which we reserve for business letters, dealings with officials, conversation with strangers and so on. As children develop, they identify with other groups of speakers by using the same forms of language as other members of those groups. They start by acquiring the dialect of whoever primarily cares for them. They adopt different roles in play, and at school rapidly learn to use language for many purposes – to amuse, to tease, to bully, to warn, to advise. As they grow, they learn to use language not only to identify with certain groups but also to exclude others. Through all of these activities they are enabled to expand their social roles, to consolidate their membership of groups, and to understand the values and attitudes of groups to which they do not belong. By an explicit study of the ways in which language is used to express social identity, at different levels of complexity, children will be better able to become effective members of a wide range of groups. It is through an increasingly flexible use of language in different situations and for different purposes that the socialisation of the child will be achieved.

Language and personal development

17.   It is not only as social beings that children will grow to take their place in society, but as private individuals, and a great deal of evidence presented to the Committee has laid stress on the importance of English for personal development: in other words, the notion that teachers of English should ensure that their pupils develop as human beings as well as communicators. The Committee accepts the view that language plays an important role both in exploring and defining responses and feelings and in shaping the kind of people we become. We would argue then that this shaping of personality and the exploration of self are inextricably bound up with language development.

18.   In practice, in the classroom, 'English for personal development' means, for example, children writing their own verse and fiction, sometimes in response to literature that they have read, shared and discussed. The notion of 'response' is important: pupils are entitled to a reading curriculum which extends their understanding of the world and themselves, and which stimulates response. Consequently, such a curriculum needs to be varied and challenging, as do the reading and writing activities that stem from such reading.

19.   Children should practise writing in a variety of forms. They should develop the ability to write clearly and accurately in Standard English. But people who would reduce English teaching to 'basics' misunderstand the nature of written language. Quite apart from all the humanistic reasons for encouraging pupils to write stories and poems, there are sound linguistic reasons, because the activity gives them the opportunity to experiment with language, trying out forms they would otherwise never use. Some of the structures of written language allow us to assemble our thoughts and to link our ideas in ways that are not so readily available in everyday spontaneous speech. Once mastered through writing, these structures are available for use in speech if the occasion demands, thereby increasing the power and flexibility of the oral repertoire. If we want children to develop their language competence to the full, we can argue against the utilitarians for the central place of a wide range of styles of writing in the language curriculum. This is simply the good practice which the best English teachers have always followed.

Children who read Tolkien and then write their own fairy stories are engaged in a total process of language development which, among other advantages, may one day contribute to the writing of clear, persuasive reports about commerce or science.

20. The Committee recognises that English teachers have an important part to play in nourishing both the intellect and the imagination. This has to be associated with technical development of an ear and eye for language, and the development of an active facility with language. All writing demands craft to ensure that the final product is readable as well as reaching to the heart of what needs to be expressed. It is not enough to write 'freely' with no thought given to the audience for the writing, or the shape and patterns of the language used. Not all writing, of course, is intended for an audience: pupils who write an immediate response to a poem in their personal journals have every right to be tentative in what they write.

Language in relation to aesthetic development

21. Aesthetic properties of language are to be found more than anywhere else in literature. Literature is nothing if not language formed in highly deliberated ways. From the earliest pre-school stages of development, children are interested in forms of language, such as the rhythms and rhymes of nursery tales, or the repetition of story structures. There is no doubt that all manner of linguistic artefacts, from the rebus of the primary class to the plays, poems, stories and essays of the 16-year-old, have a tenacious grasp on the imagination of school age children. Wide reading, and as great an experience as possible of the best imaginative literature, are essential to the full development of an ear for language, and to a full knowledge of the range of possible patterns of thought and feeling made accessible by the power and range of language. Matching book to the pupil is an aspect of the English teacher's work which requires fine judgement and sensitivity to the needs of the child. It is good for children to respond to good contemporary works, written both for children and for adults. It is equally important for them to read and hear and speak the great literature of the past. Our modern language and our modern writing have grown out of the language and literature of the past. The rhythms of our daily speech and writing are haunted not only by the rhythms of nursery rhymes, but also by the rhythms of Shakespeare, Blake, Edward Lear, Lewis Carroll, the Authorised Version of the Bible. We do not completely know what modern writing is unless we know what lies behind it. Hemingway's short sentences derive their power from their revolt against earlier, more discursive styles. *The Diary of Adrian Mole* is a descendant of Dickens's urgent, knowingly innocent style. The apparently 'free' verse of D. H. Lawrence is imbued with the rhythms of the Book of Common Prayer.

22. It is possible that a generation of children may grow up deprived of their entitlement – an introduction to the powerful and splendid history of the best that has been thought and said in our language. Too rigid a concern with what is 'relevant' to the lives of young people seems to us to pose the danger of impoverishing not only the young people, but the culture itself, which has to be revitalised by each generation.

23. As children read more, write more, discuss what they have read and move through the range of writing in English, they amass a store of images from half-remembered poems, of lines from plays, of phrases, rhythms and ideas. Such a *reception* of language allows the individual greater possibilities of *production* of language. In later years of schooling,

pupils can be brought to the point of reflecting upon literary style and its relation to a variety of values: they can begin to recognise that the language of literature is not transparent, but layered with meanings, and creates a view of the world revealed by the writing itself.

24. In the 1960s and 1970s, there was a desire to bring into the classroom urgent concerns about the relations between language, literature, politics and social conditions. But it has been argued that the result was that English lessons became in some schools no more than the setting for vigorous moral and social discussion, which too often assumed that language was a clear window onto a social world. Certain kinds of literary, journalistic and commercial manipulation might be studied, but the largely thematic discussions involved offered little analysis of rhetoric, choice of language, metaphor, vocabulary and other persuasive and argumentative devices. Still less were they concerned with the pleasures of crafting and ordering related to writing in precise forms, or studying literary genres.

25. The recent structuralist and post-structuralist revolutions in literary theory have caused people to think very energetically and critically about the relationship between the structures of language and the structures of thought, as well as the relationship between the structures of language and the structures of our culture. Today, many graduates in English are excited by and well-informed about these ideas. Some of them may become teachers in schools, and may, as a result of these interests, welcome a greater emphasis on the teaching of knowledge about language. For the central ideas of structuralism and post-structuralism do indeed spring from the study of language as the human way of ordering experience. (de Saussure's linguistic theories and Derrida's *Grammatology*, for example, offer linguistic models of thought which have subsequently been extended to anthropology, aesthetics, philosophy and the study of culture in general.)

26. It is not necessary to specialise in such studies to be aware that our ways of structuring sentences and thoughts, and, by extension, our ways of structuring our cultural values and beliefs, affect the whole of our individual and social lives. But essential to understanding and describing those effects is a greater knowledge about language than most of us have had the opportunity to acquire.

The teaching of language

27. Widely divergent views are now held on the value of the formal elements of knowledge about language. Many people believe that standards in our use of English would rise dramatically if we returned to the formal teaching of grammar which was normal practice in most classrooms before 1960. Others believe that explicit teaching or learning of language structure is unnecessary. We believe that both these extreme viewpoints are misguided. Research evidence suggests that old-fashioned formal teaching of grammar had a negligible, or, because it replaced some instruction and practice in composition, even a harmful, effect on the development of original writing. We do not recommend a return to that kind of grammar teaching. It was based on a model of language derived from Latin rather than English. However, we believe that for children not to be taught anything about language is seriously to their disadvantage.

28. Many teachers of English suspect that explicit talk about how language works may inhibit a child's natural abilities in speaking and in writing. The Bullock Report stated (Chapter 12) that, 'In general, a

curriculum subject, philosophically speaking, is a distinctive mode of analysis. While many teachers recognise that their aim is to initiate a student in a particular mode of analysis, they rarely recognise the linguistic implications of doing so'. Since the publication of the Bullock Report, many subject departments in secondary schools have moved their thinking to pay attention to this notion to the extent that the phrase 'Language across the curriculum', used to designate that movement, has been assimilated into educational jargon. But it should apply not only to subjects other than English. There is no reason why the subject of the English language should not be discussed like any other. We believe that within English as a subject, pupils need to have their attention drawn to what they are doing and why they are doing it because this is helpful to the development of their language ability. It is important, however, to state that helping pupils to notice what they are doing is a subtle process which requires the teacher to intervene constructively and at an appropriate time.

29. Awareness of the forms of language is an entirely natural development. People using language in daily life often make reference to their own language usages, and to those of others. They comment on what is said or written, discuss whether they like or dislike the form, as well as the content, of what they hear and read. People in general are curious about the workings of language, and English lessons should build on that curiosity. Children in particular are fascinated by word games – by puns, backslang, tongue-twisters, conundrums, double meanings, anagrams, palindromes, etymologies and 'secret' languages. If a move from spontaneous practice to considered reflection is sensitively handled by the teacher, it becomes quite natural to talk about language in classrooms. If a pupil keeps on omitting main verbs from sentences, it is inefficient to keep on drawing attention to specific omissions, when by understanding that there is a word class (i.e. verb), which functions as the nucleus of each sentence, the pupil can in future check the presence of a verb for himself. If a pupil is having difficulty with pronouns, scattering words such as *she* or *they* or *them* throughout a text, providing inadequate guidance as to what *she*, *they* or *them* refers to, it is clearly of importance that the pupil begin to apply a general rule of reference which implies the knowledge of the relationship of pronoun to noun. Since, therefore, teacher and pupil need, in discussion, a word which refers to a class of terms (i.e. pronouns) there is no good reason not to use that term. Teachers and pupils, in the process of editing and redrafting written work, will be helped by descriptive technical language to talk about it, using terms such as 'word', 'sentence' or 'paragraph'. Then it is likely that good progress will be made. Teaching language must involve talking about language, since learning without that activity is slow, inefficient and inequitable (in that it favours those whose ability enables them to generalise without tuition).

30. The evidence we have received stresses that these terms must be acquired mainly through an exploration of the language pupils use, rather than through exercises out of context. Pupils whose language experiences have made them confident only in personal and colloquial modes need practice in meeting a range of graduated demands, under careful guidance, with much personal support. Before 1960, it was usual to over-emphasise parts of speech, sentence structure and punctuation and to teach these through exercises unrelated to the child's real needs. There are schools where this still goes on. At the other extreme, pupils follow programmes of work in English which involve much listening, speaking,

reading and writing, in contexts and for purposes which engage their interests and extend their skill in using language, but do not exploit the learning opportunities fully because they are related to an inadequate framework of ideas about language. Information about language structure is most effectively made explicit at the moment when it is useful in real communication, so that the explicit statement consolidates the implicit awareness and effective learning occurs.

Standard English
31.   In paragraph 5 of this chapter, we spoke of the necessity for a standard language as adults move from their localised speech communities into a wider world. This must be the language which we have in common, which we call Standard English. All of us can have only partial access to Standard English: the language itself exists like a great social bank on which we all draw and to which we all contribute. As we grow older, and encounter a wider range of experience, we encounter more of the language, but none of us is ever going to know and use all the words in the Oxford English Dictionary, which is itself being constantly updated, nor are we going to produce or to encounter all possible combinations of the structures which are permissible in English. When children go to school for the first time, their language may differ in many respects from Standard English, depending on where they live, their parents' speech habits, and so on. This is natural and proper and a source of richness. However, one of the schools' duties is to enable children to acquire Standard English, which is their right. This is not a matter of controversy: no item of evidence received by the Committee contained disagreement with this point.

32.   It is important to be clear about the nature of Standard English. It developed from one of the Middle English dialects (East Midlands – the dialect first printed by Caxton) to become the written form used by all writers of English, no matter which dialect area they come from. It is the fact of being the written form which establishes it as the standard. And it is the fact of being the written form which means that it is used not only in Britain but by all writers of English throughout the world, with remarkably little variation.

33.   Since it holds this important role in the written form, it is also used to communicate across local areas and between regions in a spoken form. In its spoken form it may be pronounced with many different regional accents – e.g. Devon, Cheshire, Midlands, Northumbrian, East Anglian. And it is also spoken far beyond these islands in Australian, American, Jamaican and Indian accents, as well as by speakers using English as a foreign language and speaking it with Japanese or Brazilian or Russian accents. There is one accent of English which is used by a minority of speakers in Britain called 'Received Pronunciation', which developed in the nineteenth century in the public schools and universities and was, between the wars, particularly associated with the BBC. This accent is the standard for foreign students of English in Britain, but is not used as the model of English pronunciation in British schools, since speakers may be rightly proud of their regional pronunciation, which identifies where they come from.

34.   Dialects of English are typically spoken rather than written down. They are spoken with local, regional accents. ('Accent' refers only to features of pronunciation, whereas 'dialect' implies regular grammatical patterns and distinctive vocabulary which characterise the language of a particular area and distinguish it from its neighbours and from Standard

English.) There are no conventions for writing dialects. It is largely for this reason, and to communicate with others in the wider world, that dialect speakers also learn the standard language.

35.   Spoken language and written language both have regular patterns and forms. Most of these, of course, they have in common. There is no sentence structure in English which is incapable of being used in both speech and writing. The same is true of words. Nevertheless, the structure of these forms is influenced by the relationship between those who use them to communicate.

36.   Both speaker and listener must make assumptions about each other's attitude, vocabulary, intentions and range of reference, but they are able to change and elaborate these assumptions as a conversation proceeds. Conversation is a joint production. The spoken language is typically more allusive, put together in shorter sentences and phrases, using vaguer, less specific terms than are usually found in writing. (*I mean, you see, this sort of thing*.) This is partly because speaker and listener share a context; it is partly because they cannot check backwards or refer forwards in their discussion or description as a reader and writer can.

37.   Writers too must make assumptions about the knowledge and attitude of their readers, but they must also make provision for the fact that they are addressing someone who is not present, whose immediate reactions cannot be gauged, and for whom cross-references, connections of thought and relations of elements of language such as pronouns and verbs must be made clear and unambiguous.

38.   Forms of written language have in the past been much more extensively studied than those of speech. There has been considerable recent interest in the spoken language both among professional students of language and in the classroom, where spoken work is encouraged, discussed and indeed assessed. Our proposed model takes account of the forms and patterns of both speech and writing. Since it is a model of language *in use*, it has had to take into account the ways in which speech and writing vary according to social uses, historical development, and the relationship between intellectual and linguistic growth.

39.   In the next chapter we present a model of English. There can be no such thing as *the* model. Constant flux is inherent in the nature of language. The word 'language' is an abstraction: it subsumes all the means by which human beings communicate in vocal or written forms with each other. As human beings and their relationships change, so does their language. Moreover, because language serves as many purposes as there are needs for communication, any model of language must be, to a greater or lesser extent, *specific*.

Chapter 3 — *The model*

1. The model which follows is derived from the educational aims referred to in the previous chapter and applies to the education system of this country. It is presented in four parts. All four parts are necessary, since each is part of a whole, thus each has full significance only in relation to the other three. The Committee hopes that this model will be discussed and debated. This chapter does not and cannot reflect the depth, range and quality of the debate which has been generated within the Committee. But the structure provides a logical and motivated framework for others to be able to take possession of the model and reshape it in a fashion which enlarges the range and enhances the quality of their own knowledge about language which we hope will increase their ability to control and be sensitive to the use of the English language.

Part 1: The forms of the English language – sounds, letters, words, sentences, and how these relate to meaning
Part 2: Communication and comprehension – how speakers and writers communicate and how listeners and readers understand them
Part 3: Acquisition and development – how the child acquires and develops language
Part 4: Historical and geographical variation – how language changes over time, and how languages which are spread over territories differentiate into dialects or indeed into separate languages.

2. Each part of the model is presented as a set of statements or lists: the statements and lists are not comprehensive, they offer examples; we have made no attempt to discuss their contents in detail. This report is not a linguistics textbook and we are not suggesting that there is only one correct approach to the study of the various parts of the model. It is nevertheless the Committee's view that teachers need thoroughly to understand the shape, scope and detail of the model. Clearly, teachers with this degree of knowledge will readily make use of it in those circumstances where they consider it appropriate to the language needs of pupils – the focus of Chapter 4 – and to pupils' entitlement in terms of language experiences and subsequent achievement (Chapter 5).

3. A full description of each part of the model would inflate this report to a preposterous length. Moreover, a full description is superfluous, since what is important is the scope and shape of the model. We suggest a list of titles of books under each section and sub-section of the model (Appendix 7). We present an eclectic approach to the issues which we believe that teachers ought to be familiar with. Since we are generalising across teacher education, and across pre-service and in-service training at different levels, we have in each section suggested some titles which sometimes simplify the issues involved, as well as some titles of more technical works which provide a more detailed discussion of the issues. (In some cases the title of a book occurs under several different heads because it has a wide coverage.) Teacher trainers will select from these lists (or from others with a similar coverage) those books which are most appropriate to the teachers they are educating. Some terms used in the chapter may be unfamiliar to the general

reader. Their meanings are either made clear in the text or given in Appendix 6.

4.   The parts of the model are presented in a series of five figures (reproduced together in Appendix 8 for ease of reference when reading this chapter). The contents of the five figures constitute the model. Following each figure are notes which illustrate ways in which someone who knows about that part of the model can reflect and comment upon their contents, in an informed and productive way. References in the left-hand margin signify some of the interrelationships between different parts of the model.

Part 1: The forms of the English language

The following boxes exemplify the range of forms found in English. If forms are combined in regular patterns, following the rules and conventions of English, they yield meaningful language.

1. *speech*
   - vowel and consonant sounds
   - syllables and word stress
   - intonation and pause
   - tone of voice

2. *writing*
   - vowel and consonant letters (the alphabet)
   - spelling and punctuation
   - paragraphing and lay-out

3. *word forms*
   - inflected words (plurals, comparatives, etc.)
   - derived words (e.g. *fair, unfair*)
   - compound words (e.g. *melt-down, play-boy, mouth-watering*)
   - idioms (e.g. *put a stop to, Take care of, lose touch with*)
   - productive metaphors (e.g. *time is money; lose time, save time, spend time, waste time, run out of time*)
   - frozen metaphors (e.g. *kick the bucket, curry favour*)

4. *phrase structure and sentence structure*
   - verbs: auxiliaries, tense, aspect, mood
   - nouns: noun classes, number, gender, definiteness, pronouns, demonstratives
   - adjectives, adverbs, adjuncts, disjuncts and conjuncts
   - simple sentence structure, co-ordination, apposition
   - complex sentence structure, subordination
   - substitution and ellipsis, negation and quantification

5. *discourse structure*
   - paragraph structure, reference, deixis, anaphora, cohesion
   - theme, focus, emphasis, given and new information structure
   - boundary markers (in speech and writing)
   - lexical collocation (i.e. drawn from the same vocabulary area)

Figure 1

Illustrative notes on Figure 1

5. Someone who knows about the forms of the English language can reflect disinterestedly and illuminatingly on a range of questions, observations and problems which crop up in everyday language use. Below, we give examples to illustrate the application of knowledge of the forms listed in each of the five boxes in Figure 1.

Box 1: speech

6. Knowledge about the aspects of speech in Box 1 facilitates informed reflection and comment on:

- word pronunciation
- how to decide where to put emphasis in language used for public speaking, play-reading, reading aloud and other social activities
- understanding the rhythms of English prose, or the syllabic structure of a line of verse, how long pauses should be, where stress falls, the nature of rhymes, alliteration, assonance, etc.
- aspects of speech relating to phenomena such as tone of voice. When people say, 'It's not so much what he said but the way he said it' they are usually referring to combinations of stress, intonation, speed of utterance, huskiness and volume, and paralinguistic features such as facial expression or gesture
- the relationships between the sound structure of words and their spelling patterns.

Box 2: writing

7. A systematic appreciation of the writing system of English provides an informed basis for considering such matters as:

- the conventional range of forms for upper and lower case letters, preferred slope of such letters in handwriting, and how to construct cursive forms
- the uses of upper and lower case letters in English
- the form of the alphabet, how it relates to the pronunciation of consonants and vowels, how to use a dictionary, thesaurus, directory, concordance
- the spelling patterns of English and how much regularity there is in English spelling: sound–spelling relations in English (e.g. *hop/hope, rat/rate, sit/site*) (see Box 1); word-pattern spellings in English (e.g. electri*c*, electri*c*ity, electri*c*ian where the spelling of the stem *electric* remains the same, though *c* is pronounced differently in each word)
- the way grammatical words in English tend to have shorter spelling patterns than full lexical words which sound the same (*but/butt, by/bye, in/inn, no/know, nor/gnaw, not/knot, so/sew, to/two*, etc.)
- punctuation conventions – which word forms (Box 3) should have apostrophes or hyphens, which grammatical structures (Box 4) are conventionally marked by capital letters, full stops, commas, colons, question marks.

Box 3: word forms

8. As we move from smaller to larger linguistic structures, the range of application becomes more complex. Areas of linguistic interest informed by a knowledge of word forms include:

- the *regular* patterning of word forms in English (so that one recognises that *tsetse* is a relatively recent borrowing from another language, since it does not fit into the regular patterns)

Figure 5(1)

- the way in which regular plurals and past tenses are formed in Standard English, and the patternings among the so-called irregular forms (e.g. *drink/drank/drunk, sing/sang/sung*, or *swim/swam/swum*)
- regular patterns of spelling (and usually of meaning as well) among derived words which contain the same stem (e.g. *declaim – declamation, exclaim – exclamation, reclaim – reclamation*)
- the efficient use of dictionaries (e.g. how to look up the infinitive rather than past tense forms of verbs)

- the subtle change of meaning of a word as it forms relationships with other words or affixes (e.g. *man, manly, mannish, con-man, Superman, Man-of-the-Year, man–machine interface*)
- synonymy (e.g. *horse, steed*), antonymy (*alive, dead*), hyponymy (*rose* and *daffodil* are hyponyms of *flower*; *canary* and *blackbird* are hyponyms of *bird*)
- the ways in which compound words are formed in English (e.g. *sunrise, birth control, window-cleaner*) and the conventions applying to writing them as one word or two, and whether or not to use a hyphen
- other ways of forming words in English (e.g. partial or complete reduplication as in: *see-saw, bow-wow, hotch-potch, higgledy-piggledy, wishy-washy, yoyo, papa, tittle-tattle, KitKat* and other names for new products)
- the use of common metaphors in newspaper headlines
- mixing metaphors
- punning, quips and word-games.

Box 4: phrase structure and sentence structure

9.   There are two principal ways in which knowledge of phrase structure and sentence structure is useful. One is the more precise expression such knowledge permits, particularly in writing. The other is the increased perception of what is meant when something is read or heard – ambiguities and uncertainties are more easily distinguished. In both cases, a clear knowledge of structure increases possibilities of subtler expression and understanding of language. Familiarity with the syntactic concerns of Box 4 allows one to address with confidence such problems and issues as the following:

- what it is that is enclosed between a capital letter and a full stop
- what a verb is and its function in a sentence

Figure 5(2)
- the control of number agreement between subject and verb (compare *they was coming* and *they were coming*)
- how adjectives are ordered in front of a noun: e.g. how it is that we can say *a small grey stone house*, but would be unlikely to say *a stone small grey house*
- the choice of the appropriate verb forms to express complex temporal and intentional relationships (e.g. *Even if it should snow on Friday, I shall still have got my potatoes in*)
- the use of modal verbs (*can/could, may/might, shall/should, will/would*)
- the patterns of prepositional meaning (e.g. motion *to, at, away from*)
- how putting an adverbial in different places in the sentence creates differences in meaning (compare *Really, she was annoyed* and *She was really annoyed*)

Figure 3
- why sentences like *No programming error is too trivial to be ignored* or *She gave him far less interesting information* make it difficult to be sure that one has interpreted them correctly
- the relationship of sentence form to sentence function (e.g. how the various interrogative forms may be used to ask different sorts of questions with different presuppositions)
- the relationship and uses of different sentence forms all of which 'say the same thing' (e.g. *John kicked the ball, The ball was kicked by John, It was John who kicked the ball, What happened to the ball was that John kicked it*)
- the relationship between direct and indirect speech, and the different kinds of indirect speech which may be exploited by an author.

Box 5: discourse structure

10.   Until a couple of decades ago, most students of the forms of language restricted themselves to considering the structure of units of language no longer than the sentence. But a large corpus of literature now exists on the structure of discourse, by which we mean a connected stretch of either speech or writing which is larger in extent than a sentence. Questions such as 'How do we understand the use of language in a particular sentence?' give rise to analysis of discourse – its nature, its forms, the devices used to make it coherent, the conventions which govern its structure, etc. A paragraph is a discourse unit in English. A systematic knowledge of discourse structure can inform responses to such topics as the following:

- how different types of paragraphs are formed

- how to make clear what it is that is being talked about (to be clear what the reference is)

- unambiguous use of referring expressions (compare *Two cars were coming down the road and one turned in front of the other one* with *Two cars were coming down the road. The one on the left turned in front of the other one*)

- the exploitation and recognition of ambiguity

- determining where to put the focus (intonation peak – see Box 1) in reading a text aloud (for instance, a part in a play). There are regular patterns of focussing: thus in answer to the question *What happened today?* a child might reply *Tom washed the DISHES* with the focus on *DISHES*. However, if the question was *Who washed the dishes?* the child would have to adjust the focus and place it on the part of the utterance which says something new, thus *TOM washed the dishes* (or, indeed, *TOM washed them, TOM did them, TOM did*, or simply, *TOM*). Once 'dishes' has been mentioned by the first speaker, it will be treated as 'given' by the second speaker

- appropriate use of indefinite and definite expressions (e.g. in a text beginning *A man was suspected of planting an explosive device*, later reference to the same man or to the same explosive device will normally be in terms of definite expressions: *the man*, the device)

- the appropriate use of conjuncts to show how the next clause relates to what has already been said (*though, however, so, besides*, etc.)

- boundary markers in different types of discourse – opening and closing of conversations, how you know when it is your turn to speak in conversation, openings and closings of different discourse types (e.g. *Once upon a time . . ., I hereby bequeath, dispose and dispone . . .*, and *They all lived happily ever after, Amen*)

- the patterning (collocation) of words from the same lexical field in many types of discourse. For example, in a recipe – words referring to ingredients and modes of cooking; in discussion of medicine – medical terminology; in planning where to go on holiday – vocabulary to do with places, times, travelling costs, amenities, leisure activities; in a headteacher's annual report, vocabulary concerned with what people do at school, and with many ways of talking about success, will be expected; in a report on the study of language forms, vocabulary connected with structure and relationships is expected.

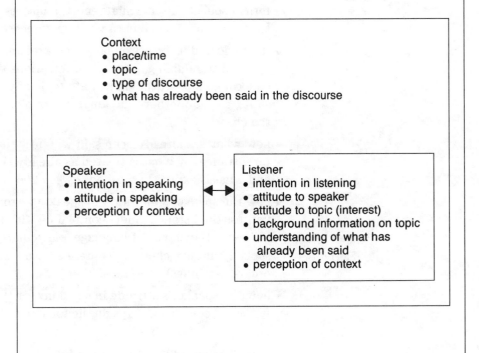

Part 2(i): Communication

Speakers and writers adapt their language to the context in which the language is being used. The boxes below indicate some of the main features of context which are relevant in conversations where the speaker and listener are talking face to face. In this section we shall also indicate how this model needs to be adapted to account for written language. (Note that in literature we often find *representations* of speech which rely on our experience of the spoken language.)

Context
- place/time
- topic
- type of discourse
- what has already been said in the discourse

Speaker
- intention in speaking
- attitude in speaking
- perception of context

Listener
- intention in listening
- attitude to speaker
- attitude to topic (interest)
- background information on topic
- understanding of what has already been said
- perception of context

Figure 2

Illustrative notes on Figure 2

11.   Someone with an informed understanding of the complex ways in which *context* affects our use of language, the way we *choose* expressions in speaking and the ways in which we *understand* when listening can comment in an unprejudiced and illuminating way on problems, questions and observations about communication and comprehension.

12.   We give below some examples to illustrate the applications of such knowledge for the boxes in this second part of the model, which relate to SPEAKER (WRITER) and LISTENER (READER). Since we are talking about the *choice of language by the speaker and the way the speaker understands* we shall often refer back to the boxes in Figure 1. However, in order to avoid tedious repetition we note here that the contextual variables in Figure 2

Figure 1 Box 1   will affect, for instance, whether the speaker speaks more or less loudly, distinctly, angrily; with more or less of a local accent; selects from one area of the vocabulary rather than another (technical terms versus lay terms,

Figure 1 Box 3   medical terms versus legal terms, local dialect words rather than Standard English words); 'high style vocabulary' (e.g. 'parsimonious') rather than 'plain style' (e.g. 'mean') or local slang; selects simple or more complex

Figure 1 Box 4   syntactic structures; chooses appropriate Standard English or local dialect

Figure 1 Box 5   constructions for the types of discourse which emerge from the interaction of all these variables – types such as conversation, public speech, prayer, reprimand, football report, joke.

SPEAKER – language variation in relation to context

13.   This permits consideration of:

- how language varies according to where the speaker is: in the classroom, in the playground, in church, at a concert, on the stage, at home, on the football field, in the doctor's surgery, at a school parents' evening, in a political meeting

- how language varies according to whether it is the beginning or end of the interaction (openings versus closings, greetings versus farewells), and how much time the speaker (or the listener) has (an extended account versus a summary)

Figure 1 Box 5

- how language varies according to the type of discourse – for instance, a formal speech, an informal report, a discussion, a greeting, a bed-time story, an announcement, a weather-forecast

- the topic and its effect on language – technical professional topics as opposed to rambling, gossipy conversations where the general topic may be local gossip but the immediate topic of conversation constantly shifts, as yet another individual (or couple, or group) is introduced into the chat

- how what has already been said will influence what can later be said – for instance, by what is treated as already shared, 'given' information, and what is explicitly recalled (*as you/I/we were saying* . . .)

Figure 1 Box 1
Fig 1 Box 4

- how the speaker's intention in speaking – to amuse, inform, persuade, impress the listener, chide, complain – with reference to the topic, will influence the choice of language, particularly how what is said is spoken but also, choice of sentence form (asking questions, giving orders, warnings)

- how the speaker's attitude in speaking (or the attitude the speaker wishes to convey, perhaps duplicitously) will influence tone of voice, and choice of words, etc.

- how the speaker's perception of the listener as 'one of the same group' or 'one of a different group', the same or a different generation, subordinate or having power, a dialect speaker or a speaker of Standard English, friendly or unfriendly, will all influence the way the speaker chooses forms of language. Finally, whether who is listening is one person, a small group, or a very large audience, will also affect the speaker's choice of language.

WRITER – language variation in relation to context

14.   Part 2 of the model specifically represents a context in which a speaker is addressing a listener. Much of this will transfer directly to a writer addressing one or more readers. We should observe, however, that in the written forms of the language, the writer's intention to some extent depends on the topic, typically more formal than the spoken language. There are some features of informal speech which it is difficult to represent accurately in writing: there are conventional written representations of the spoken forms of *cannot* (*can't*), *I am* (*I'm*), etc. but not of other very frequent forms like the normal spoken weak forms of *supposed to* (?sposta), *I am going to* (?angona), *already, all right, although* (?oready, ?oright, ?orthough).

15.   Furthermore, whereas language may be spoken with an accent which informs the listener where the speaker comes from and also gives some indication of class, social affiliation, etc. and also may be spoken with dialect words and dialect syntax, in the written language it is not common to find these features represented, and so, since there are often

no conventional written representations of these features, in written language we usually find Standard English being used.

16.   Someone who fully appreciates the different requirements of spoken and written language can comment on, for instance:

- how writers have to remember that they are writing for readers who are not present at the time of writing. The reader cannot see what the writer sees, and cannot share the writer's immediate preoccupations at the time the writer experiences them. The fact of writing for an absent reader normally requires much more specific, less allusive forms of expression than those which a speaker can use

- how the effects of topic, what has already been written, the writer's intentions in writing, the writer's attitude towards the reader, will all have the same sort of effect on the writer's choice of language as they have on the speaker's choice

- the types of discourse available to a writer are of course different from those available to a speaker, since the mode of composition can be sustained for much longer (put aside and then taken up again), allowing time for reflection and redrafting, and can be undertaken in co-operation with other writers. In general, the conventions of written language require selection of more formal vocabulary than is commonly used in spoken language, and the written language readily permits the expression of complex ideas and relationships where complex syntactic structures will be required – structures which might have to be simplified if expressed in spoken language

- a speaker may monitor the effect of what he or she is saying, and constantly adjust what is being said so that it is more comprehensible to the listener. This immediacy of response is denied the writer, who has to make an effort of imagination to understand what the reader will find difficult, and has to foresee what the reader may misunderstand because the language may be ambiguous or unclear

- how spoken language is typically reciprocal, so that the speaking turn alternates – hence the joint achievement of talk.

Part 2 (ii): Comprehension – some processes of understanding

In Figure 2 we showed the context of communication which is of course the context in which comprehension takes place. We understand language in a context of use. Some of the processes involved in understanding are indicated in this figure which, like Figure 2, is orientated to the speaker/listener relationship; in the notes on this section we shall show how these figures can be adapted to give an account of reading with understanding.

1. interpreting speech sounds (Figure 1, Box 1) as words and phrases (Figure 1, Boxes 3 and 4), working out the relevant relations of these (Figure 4) and deriving a 'thin' meaning of the sort that a sentence might have out of context

2. working out what the speaker is using phrases *to refer to* in the world or in the previous discourse

3. working out from the form of the utterance what the speaker presupposes in making the utterance

4. inferring what the speaker means by making a particular utterance at a particular point in the discourse – the 'thick pragmatic meaning'

(All of these processes may apply simultaneously)

Figure 3

Illustrative notes on Figure 3 LISTENER

17. Someone with a good grasp of the forms of language (Figure 1), the way that language is understood in a context (Figure 2) and the processes of language understanding (Figure 3) can reflect and comment illuminatingly on problems, questions and observations to do with language understanding which crop up in everyday life. Again, examples of such problems and issues include:

Figure 1 Box 1 • why a speaker sounds boring and fails to rouse the listener's interests

Figure 1 Box 1 • why a speaker does not sound sincere in what he or she says

Figure 1 Box 1
Figure 3 Box 1 • why two listeners may disagree about what was actually said (since the
Figure 2 phonetic details of speech are often obscure or because the listeners' expectations of what they would hear were different)

• why one interpretation of what was said is more likely than another, given the *context* – for example, the sort of person the speaker is, previous expressions of belief by the speaker, how the listener might have been influenced by a particular knowledge of the topic the speaker was talking
Figure 2 about, or from what was said immediately before or immediately after the utterance at issue

Figure 2
Figure 3 Box 2

- how two listeners may disagree in their understanding of what is being talked about since the speaker has failed to make his or her referring expressions sufficiently clear (perhaps because the different states of knowledge about the topic of the two listeners have not been sufficiently taken into account)

- why the person addressed feels frustrated and indignant but does not quite understand how to refute a presupposition that is not directly asserted. If a speaker says 'So you didn't hit him' it can only be said in a context where someone (perhaps the speaker) has supposed that you did

- how to relate two utterances where the relationship between them is not made explicit by the speaker. In the utterances 'Mr X's wife is still missing. Police are digging in the garden now' the relationship between the two statements demands a number of inferences based on knowledge of the world: that Mr X's wife has already been missing for some time (a presupposition encoded in *still*) – that to say someone has been missing for some time often means that they have been killed – that many killings are domestic – that bodies are often found close to where they have been killed – that 'the garden' mentioned here is likely to be 'Mr X's garden' because the hypothesis is that he has killed his wife – and that one digs in a garden to find a body that may have been buried there . . . – where if any part of this is not part of the cultural or background knowledge of the listener, the listener may find difficulty in understanding the implications of what is hinted at here, hence in drawing the necessary inferences to determine what the speaker means but does not actually say.

READER   18.   This is useful in the following ways:

- noting that, just as in listening, the reader will be influenced in interpretation by: who the writer is (or purports to be) – a public authority, an extremist organisation, a distinguished author, a local resident, a 14-year-old, the bank manager, a much loved relation; the writer's apparent intention in writing – to advise, apologise, express devotion, inform, amuse; the topic – man's inhumanity to man, 'my pet', the voyages of Columbus, the state of the current bank account; the type of discourse – a sonnet, an essay, a letter, a scribbled message, a newspaper review column, a report, a novel; and what has already been written in the discourse

- being aware of how the discourse which the writer creates may owe much to the external context in which the writer writes (e.g. political comment) in which case the *here and now* of the writing may have a powerful influence on the choices of language made. Or the writer may be concerned to express eternal truths in a literary form, in which case the external context may be less relevant and the relevant context will be *that created by the writing*. This creation of context as an imaginary or eternal world *within the discourse* is a particularly characteristic feature of literary writing

- taking heed that the reader does not, of course, share the context of utterance with the writer but must make an imaginative effort to recreate the context: the more distant in time or space, or the more unfamiliar the context which has shaped the writer's message, the greater the difficulty the reader will have in understanding (and being sure of having reached the correct understanding) of what the writer wished to communicate

- explaining to oneself and possibly to others how literary writers often exploit the resources of the language to fuse two different points of view in a narrative. In the following extract from a novel – 'She was desperately anxious . . . that on this morning things should go well. Today a lot was at stake', the narrator tells about what happened in the past (*was* anxious, *was* at stake) but the anxiety seems to be experienced by the character at the time of the experience (*this* morning, *today*)

Figure 1 Boxes 4–5

- discussing how 'a literary context' affects the reader's disposition to create a rich interpretation. For instance, in reading poetry the reader may pause to allow an image to expand in the mind and to resonate with a range of previously experienced images, encouraging a process which would be inappropriate on such a scale in reading a bus timetable or instructions for erecting a tent.

Figure 2

> **Part 3: Acquisition and development**
>
> 1. Children gradually acquire the forms of language identified in the boxes of Figure 1. Whereas some aspects of acquisition are fairly rapid (most children have acquired a full range of vowels and consonants by the time they are 6 or 7), other aspects develop much later (for example, control of spelling patterns and conventions of punctuation).
>
> ───────────────────────────────
>
> 2. Children gradually develop their ability to produce and to understand appropriate forms of language (both spoken and written) in a wide range of contexts (Figure 2). This development does not cease in the years of schooling but continues throughout life.

Figure 4

Illustrative notes on Figure 4

19.   Someone who has a sound knowledge of the typical progression in learning to use language can distinguish between a *normal* pattern of development (with a normal range of early and late developers, fast and slow developers) and an *abnormal* pattern which indicates that a child may need special help. This is clearly of importance to teachers, in both the primary and secondary phases of education, as well as to parents and all those concerned with the development of young people. Some of the most important applications of knowledge of language acquisition and development are:

Figure 1 Boxes 3–5

- distinguishing between what is difficult for a child at a particular stage to produce and to understand and what is easy (for instance, not only difficult vocabulary or sentence structures which many teenagers still have problems with, but also some discourse types). Simple co-operative conversation, simple narratives or simple instructions may not be difficult for younger children but other discourse types (reasoned argument, justification, explanation or complex narratives involving several participants and overlapping times of action) may prove difficult for many children well into the years of secondary schooling

Figure 2

- helping a child to make explicit what he or she is trying to say and, even more, to write – where there is a strong tendency, particularly among children, to assume that what the speaker knows is, at least to some extent, already known to the listener or reader

Figure 3

- recognising where a child's inexperience will be such that the child cannot 'fill in' the inferences required to understand a particular discourse – at least not in the same way that an adult with wider relevant experience might understand it. In the statement 'Among them were the Secretary of State, Mr Alexander Haig, the Chairman of the Federal Reserve Board, Mr Paul Volcker, and a senior member of the National Security Council' are there three people mentioned here or five? Only knowledge of the world permits the reader to be sure (from Perera (1984), p.293).

Figure 5

Illustrative notes on Figure 5

20. Someone who is knowledgeable about the process of language change, and in particular the history of English, can reflect and comment illuminatingly on such matters as:

- the ways in which Standard English has evolved from Middle English dialects

- the ways in which meanings of words change over time. For example, in Coleridge's *The Ancient Mariner*, the 'silly buckets on the deck' were not stupid but rather 'vacant' and in that context had overtones of innocence. The word *silly* has evolved from Old English *sælig* (holy) through meanings of 'innocent', 'naïve', 'unworldly', 'foolish' to its present meaning

Figure 1 Box 4

- the retention of forms in some dialects which have disappeared from Standard English (*thee/tha* in Yorkshire, the possessive structure *the man that his wife's dead* in Northumberland)

- the reasons why there are many more and much greater dialect variations in English within the British Isles than there are in, say, Australia

Figure 1 Box 3

- the ways in which Standard English has borrowed words and structures (and even discourse types, e.g. the sonnet) from other languages, and borrows them still (*sputnik, discotheque*)

Figure 1 Box 4

- the systematic ways in which the grammar of some dialects differs from the grammar of Standard English

    Standard English: *he was/they were*
    East Anglian: *he was/they was*
    South Western: *he were/they were*

- the ways in which, historically and currently, groups settling in Britain have enriched English (and created a multi-lingual community in which many languages other than English, Welsh and Gaelic now subsist side by side – Polish, Ukrainian, Urdu, Gujerati, Afro-Caribbean creole languages, Cantonese, Turkish, and so on)

Figure 1 Box 4

- the systematic ways in which the grammars of some Afro-Caribbean creole languages differ from the grammar of Standard English (even though much of the vocabulary may overlap), e.g. the absence of the verb 'to be' in simple sentences: *I going now* (Standard English *I am going now*); *The ground dry* (Standard English *The ground is dry*). Subject pronouns having the same form as object pronouns: *Me have two brothers* (Standard English *I have two brothers*); *Him gone* (Standard English *He's gone*)

30

Figure 1 Box 4   • how certain prepositional phrases frequently occurring in speech (hence
                     in the writing of some pupils) are dialectal forms rather than 'bad
                     grammar'

                     I looked *out* the window (Standard English *out of*)

                     We got *off of* the bus (Standard English *off*)

                     She asked the two *on* us (Standard English *of*)

                     We're going *up* the park (Standard English *to*)

                   • the reasons why a number of different standard forms of English have
                     emerged (Standard Indian English, Standard American English,
                     Standard Nigerian English) and how closely they are related to
                     Standard English, particularly in the written form

                   • the use of the English language throughout the world as a mother-
                     tongue, a second language and as a foreign language.

21.   This is the model of the English language, in outline only, knowledge
of which the Committee sees as both desirable and necessary for all
teachers of English and all teachers of primary school children.

**The Committee recommends that the model required by the first
term of reference be that presented in this report.**

Chapter 4 Teacher and pupil: The model in use

1. It is the purpose of this chapter to illustrate the relevance of the language model to English teaching throughout the school age-range and beyond. By giving illustration of classroom activities, we shall get closer to answering the question: 'How does all this help the teacher and, through the teacher, the children and our future adult population?'

2. Children arrive at their first school able to use at least their own spoken language. But this ability varies widely from child to child. The best start for a pre-school child is where parents and others attend to what the child is saying to them and respond appropriately; where parents and children talk to each other in some kind of shared enterprise; where the child is increasingly encouraged to become aware that talk is something you do to serve a need, for a distinct purpose; where the adult makes time available to talk; where words are played with as a matter of habit; and where games, rhymes and routines are 'language focussed'. Young children's verbal abilities are stretched and made more flexible by challenge and involvement, by new and different contexts and circumstances for talk. But we are well aware that not all homes are part of such a world. However, that reinforces the need for schools to prepare their pupils for parenthood.

Writing and reading
Writing

3. It is in the nature of school life to have to struggle to make one's meanings clear to others, even if only to a teacher. The use of language to clarify one's own feelings and thought, the kind of fumbling, tentative groping for meaning, is of utmost importance in school learning, as it is throughout life. Pedagogically, it is important for the teacher to be able to distinguish and accept such tentative language as a stage on the path to clearer expression. In this area there is now a welcome tendency in English lessons towards, for example, redrafting, when written work, after discussion, is re-worked and improved, as are many important pieces of writing in later life (although rewriting can become a dull and ill-understood exercise unless sensitively and knowledgeably directed). For the discussion of the first draft to be helpful, teacher and pupil need to be able to use a shared vocabulary for talking about writing. There is much more to writing than spelling and punctuation. Is it clear, in general, what the writer is writing about – is 'the topic' clearly identified? Is it clear who the participants are – is 'the referent' in each case clearly identified? Would it be clearer to use a richer 'adjective' or a different 'noun'? Is there 'a sentence' which seems to be too long – what makes it too long and how might the problem be remedied? Is there 'a paragraph' which is too long – what makes it too long and what makes you decide to break a paragraph in one place rather than another? Is there an expression which jars, which does not seem to fit in very well – is there 'a synonym' which would suit this type of writing better? If the writing is a rather repetitive account of a football match, would it be brightened by putting in some description of the crowd, or the day, or the field – where would the description best go? It is hard for all of us to see the faults of what we have just written unless we can leave the writing alone for a time, and then come back to it with fresh eyes. The teacher

will rarely have time to work in detail with each pupil on the improvement of a piece of writing: the neighbouring pupil, however, can be an ideal editor as long as this pupil knows how to respond with constructive advice that goes beyond just spelling and punctuation. If the teacher is to help children to improve their skills in reading, or in speaking, it will not be sufficient for the teacher alone to be aware of the formal and functional characteristics of different types of language use: the pupils must share this knowledge so that they can use it in developing their own and one another's competence.

Example i: a 7-year-old

4. If children's writing is to develop, we must discern their strengths as well as their weaknesses. Here is a record of a simple experience by a girl aged 7

Yesterday we went out for walk and We walked over some bridges and we saw some workmen and we went passed our house and Mrs Brown said that our gardon was nice and we crossed the riverban and we went up mud lane and we saw sugar my partner was Joanne and when we came back it was playtime. (Ann)

5. Ann has a vivid way with narrative. Her account moves irresistibly forward. She already has some grasp of sentence variation – '*when* we came back it was playtime.'. She uses capitals properly for the obvious proper nouns (*Mrs Brown, Joanne*), but not for what may be in her perception common nouns (*sugar, mud lane*). Her spelling errors show that she has begun to comprehend the patterns of English spelling. But this is the work of a 7-year-old. As Ann progresses she will learn about the placing of full stops. She will see how events can be given different prominence by varying the sentence pattern – 'We went up Mud Lane *where* we saw Sugar'. Building on what the child already grasps, the teacher will help her forward, perhaps initially by encouraging a second draft with some restructuring of her narrative.

6. Such guidance will draw upon and extend Ann's discernible practice, starting from what she can achieve, not from an externally imposed notion of development enforced by a course book and its drills. We cannot say how many improving techniques Ann might assimilate at once, but making some of them will contribute directly to her writing development. Sadly, the HMI survey *Primary Education in England* (1978, p. 50) found that 'in only about a third of the classes were samples of children's written work regularly used to monitor their progress' and that 'in fewer than half of the classes was children's own written work used as a basis for teaching spelling, syntax, sentence structure or style'.

Example ii: a 15-year-old

7. A contrasting example is given by a 15-year-old's account of something interesting learned in a history lesson. The theme of the lesson had concerned nutrition at the time of the industrial revolution.

But what people eat to day
is about 4 times as what they
had eaten in one day And once
they asked what is for dinner and
the reply is potatoes they start
to moan
(Brian)

The Committee does not offer this example of Brian's work as a typical example of 15-year-olds' writing, but to demonstrate further how knowledge about language on the part of the teacher might be applied in the consideration of pupils' writing.

8.   What people would notice first about this (or any) text is the orthographic shapes – the spelling, the punctuation, the general layout. In this instance, there are two things to notice. The spelling is unexceptionable: the punctuation deviates from standard usage in two respects. There is no full stop after *had eaten in one day* (though the following word *And* begins with a capital letter) and there are no quotation marks (or 'speech marks') around *what is for dinner* (the phrase should conformably have been written 'What is for dinner?') and *potatoes* (as 'Potatoes!(.)'). Either that, or the tense forms are wrong (see below). It may be that a teacher would regard these as merely careless omissions. There is nothing amiss with the word structure: it is clear that the pupil can inflect participles (*eaten*) and can form plurals (*potatoes*), though the word choices are very simple, with only three words requiring any kind of modification from the simple stem form (*eaten*, *asked*, *potatoes*). However, when we begin to look at the phrase and sentence structure, there is more to comment on. First, the tense forms have gone awry. In the first sentence the pronoun *they*, although syntactically referring to *people* in line 1, is obviously meant to refer to people of a former age. Possibly because of a confusion caused by the misuse of the pronouns, the form *had eaten* in line 3 should have read 'used to eat'. In the second sentence, if the given punctuation is retained, then *is* should have been *was*, and *start* should have been *started*. So, either the punctuation or the tense choice is wrong. At a different level, the use of *today* in line 1 requires a second and contrasting temporal adverb after *in one day* (especially in view of the word repetition involved in the choice of *in one day* rather than 'in 24 hours', or 'during the same period' or some other synonymous phrase). There is a potential ambiguity in the use of *once* in line 3. 'Once' can mean either 'on one particular occasion', or 'as soon as', depending on its syntactic function. It may be obvious that in this context the latter meaning is intended, but the next time the pupil uses it it may not be so clear, and so the potential ambiguity is worth pointing out. The use of the word *moan* is also ambiguous. If *moan* is taken literally, we are to understand that people made low-pitched sounds of distress; again, in the particular context it is obviously more likely to mean simply *complain*. In this extract, a colloquial synonym for *complain* has been used in a context where stylistically a non-colloquial synonym is required. If we are to encourage children to use language with precision and care, the possible clashes of meaning should be made explicit. The extract as a whole, then, shows a command of Standard English, but has a number of weaknesses. The teacher must decide what to comment on and the extent to which technical terms would be useful. That depends on his or her knowledge of the individual author, as well as what one can typically expect of a 15-year-old who is engaged in writing a narrative account of social differences in a historical context.

9.   Drawing together the various aspects of linguistic knowledge required of the teacher, we see from the above that at least the following aspects are relevant:

- punctuation and its relationship with meaning
- use of pronouns
- structure of phrase and sentence, including choice of verb tenses and choice of adverbial expressions
- word choice in relation to word meaning and appropriateness to context
- knowledge of discourse types in writing
- knowledge of language acquisition and development.

Of course, a teacher possessing the kinds of knowledge listed would still need a good deal more, including a developing understanding of individual pupils' tendencies, weaknesses and strengths, a clear notion of the place of the exercise in an overall teaching scheme, the ability to organise time to allow for comment to the pupil on those points considered to be important – in general, pedagogic as well as linguistic expertise.

10.   It is not only in the area of linguistic form that the teacher's knowledge about language is applicable. Extending and refining vocabulary is central to development throughout the whole school age-range, and this can be made more effective by knowing about the lexical relationships of English. One way of applying such knowledge could be by exploring with pupils such matters as synonymy: with younger children it may be profitable to consider how, for example, smallness can best be expressed in different contexts – just when one might or might not use *small, little, minute, minuscule, tiny, wee*. Indeed, explicit attention to words and their meanings should be integral to English teaching throughout school life. In one secondary classroom we visited, the class encountered the word 'selfless'. None of the pupils could guess what it meant and a discussion followed without recourse to a dictionary, which left the meaning of the word obscure. An opportunity was missed here to relate *selfless* to *selfish*, and to relate *selfless* to other words with -*less* suffixes – *careless, charmless, mindless*. Similarly, explaining the differences between formal and informal usage, or comparing Standard English words with localised dialect words, or explaining the retention in dialects of otherwise obsolete forms (*thee, thou/tha*) may be enhanced by a knowledge of lexical development and relationships. In a class in which different first languages are spoken, much curiosity can be aroused by comparing different usages. Systematic stress laid upon the regularity of usages is a step on the way to linguistic tolerance. And historical perspectives can be introduced with benefits of many kinds. They can be introduced with enormous benefit in order to develop an awareness and understanding of changes in the language which are taking place in our own time. They can also aid social acceptance of speech habits and dialects which are different from the child's own.

Example iii: a 6-year-old

11.   Christine (aged 6 years 7 months) has watched the television series *How We Used to Live* and discussed it in class with her teacher; her teacher had decided that a first-person narration was appropriate for Christine's writing assignment which resulted in the following:

One morning I woke-up and felt cold because I only had rags on. I got dressed. I wore a skirt and belly-clout. I had to rock the baby and get water from the well and get the breakfast ready. So I gave the cradle a push and the baby went to sleep. Then I went down stairs to go and get breakfast ready. I saw the pot was there all-ready hanging over the fire. I put the oats in the water. My brother came in with the wood and put it under the pot. Then my brother lit the fire with a tinder box. The water bubbled in the pot with the fire under neath. I mixed the porridge with a big wooden spoon. So the family sat down and had their porridge.

12.   Using the first-person narrative has helped Christine both to understand and to enter imaginatively into the social conditions of the poor *Three Hundred Years Ago* (her title). It has helped her to assimilate detail (*belly-clout, tinder box, pot* and *fire*), reflected in her accurate choice of words, and to focus on and to write vividly about a way of life which is outside her experience. She is beginning to be able to express complex relationships by using subordinate clauses and qualifying phrases

(*because . . . , so . . . , then . . . , with the fire under neath,* and so on).
She is experimenting with word formation and punctuation (*all-ready, under neath*) and is confident in her use of the past tense. Here, a knowledge both of forms of language and of language acquisition can enable the teacher to recognise and appreciate Christine's remarkable achievements and to encourage her to make further progress.

13.   It is important that young writers learn to make their own decisions and choices about content, style, tone and appropriate language. In making their own newspapers, radio broadcasts or television news bulletins, they will need to discuss explicitly a whole range of language issues. These are not confined to syntax and lexis; pupils will soon realise that a news story has a different impact according to the order in which the facts (or even the pictures) are arranged. Word processors are useful here. Pupils producing newspapers are keen to ensure that the product looks convincing. The word processor, with its ability to shape, delete and move text around, provides the means by which pupils can achieve a satisfactory product. Software which convincingly replicates the format of newspapers is becoming increasingly available. Through the use of word processors pupils are drawn into explicit discussion of the nature and likely impact of what they write. They will begin to talk about appropriate structure, correct punctuation and spelling and the vocabulary appropriate for their audience. The process of writing – redrafting through editing to proof-reading and publishing – is one which children take to with enjoyment.

Reading   14.   The importance of the interrelationship betwen reading and writing is most evident when we come to literature. Indeed, the teaching of literature brings together all four modes of language. We assume that in the classroom pupils are reading books, plays and poems, singly, in groups, or as a whole class; that they are reading aloud, sharing and listening to readings; that they are discussing what they are reading, establishing meaning, considering content and assessing effects.

15.   The nature of their response, in speech and writing, will depend on their age, the text, and the teacher's plan for the lesson or sequence of lessons. As they read more thoroughly, pupils should be helped to look not only at ideas and meaning but at how meaning is expressed and at effects achieved in writing. They may want to consider, for instance, the length and shape of sentences, punctuation choices, effects of emphasis, repetition, stress and intonation, ambiguities which may be lexical or structural. The teacher's knowledge of the tools of analysis, linguistic and literary, should be confident and comprehensive. *It is for the teacher to decide how much of that knowledge is made explicit to a pupil or class at a given moment, and how it might be done.* It could be planned as part of a lesson or unit of lessons, or a point may arise incidentally and explanation then seem appropriate and useful. Without such developing language knowledge, the implicit gradually becoming explicit and articulated, a child's capacity for intelligent reading and for reflection upon what is read will be restricted.

16.   Some teachers of literature whom we saw at work told us that they were sceptical of 'knowledge about language' in the English lesson, though often, in fact, they were making use of such knowledge. Their opposition was based partly on uncertainties of definition and partly on memories of past bad practices. They feared that literature might be used merely as a means of 'teaching language', that literature might be used as

material for exercises, comprehension questions about word functions, or banal memory tests. They foresaw the mechanical application of lists or learnt technical terms to texts, a practice which they rejected. The Committee, too, rejects such practices, while insisting that a sound application of knowledge about language to texts read in school increases understanding and pleasure.

Some examples – pupils

17.   A class of 10-year-olds have been reading limericks and the teacher has asked them to try writing some themselves. She is writing too. She knows that the metrical form works through a fixed pattern, involving a given number of lines, length of lines, rhyme, rhythm and stress, positioning of subject, and joke in the last line. She understands the clear patterns of reader-listener expectation. Ear well attuned, the teacher may be able to produce several good limericks without engaging in further analysis. But it is unlikely that the children will be able to do this. They will need help in discovering the essentials of the verse structure and they may need to count syllables and beat stresses and mark rhyme schemes as well as think of a good joke line. Reading and writing ballads involves the same attention to form as well as content. Children who write poetry, to judge by what has been published in anthologies and competitions in recent years, show a continuing preference for free verse and seldom use stanzaic or any forms. It is understandable that teachers encouraged the abandoning of forced rhymes and mechanical rhythms, but much that is valuable has been lost. Both professional poets and tentative beginners can be led to felicitous discoveries of new words and phrases (and even thoughts) by the exigencies of rhyme. Real poems often begin with a cadence or a form, before the 'content' is known at all.

18.   A third-year secondary school class are reading a poem by e. e. cummings – 'anyone lived in a pretty how town'. There are puzzles in the poem. The teacher knows that the meaning goes beyond what is paraphrasable and she does not want to get between the poem and the readers. But she decides that the pleasure and understanding of the poem involve an awareness of e. e. cummings's use of language. Talking about what is unusual or unexpected about the language may follow discussion and creative response or may lead into these. But well handled, it will be rewarding and illuminating. It will not 'spoil' the poem or extinguish the sense of discovery and excitement that its rhythm and story have evoked. By considering the syntactic shifts, the way in which members of one word class are violently dislocated to a different word class (verb to noun, adjective to verb, etc.), an exciting and informative lesson is generated.

19.   These lines from *Macbeth* require decisions about meaning which involve structure and word function:

> . . . No, this my hand will rather
> The multitudinous seas incarnadine,
> Making the green one red.

Any actor has to make a decision before he speaks the lines on the stage. In the last line, does 'one' refer to the sea, with 'green' and 'red' as adjectives describing the colour of the sea before and after? If so, there will be a pause after 'one' and a stress on both 'green' and 'red'. Or is 'green' a noun, 'the green' referring elliptically to the green sea, with 'one' functioning as an adverb modifying 'red' i.e. wholly or entirely red, in which case 'one' and 'red' will have equal stress? Reading these lines closely, a thoughtful student will also respond to the effect of the contrast between the last two lines, and at the same time seek a vocabulary to express precisely what is there: an interplay between the

Latin-derived polysyllables of 'multitudinous seas incarnadine', with all the effects of sound (wave-like intonation pattern?) and association they carry, and the plain English words which force home the harsh, inescapable truth to Macbeth, all expressed in a syntactically ambiguous way.

Some examples – older pupils and student teachers

20.   In offering the examples described in the next few paragraphs the Committee is well aware that it has offered texts which, in the main, are read by able, older children. We would suggest that teachers during their initial training could usefully consider them and discuss how the issues raised can inform their future teaching. As children mature, acquire more experience of the world (including its linguistic behaviour) and come to read more complex language, their need for a knowledge about language increases.

21.   Precise knowledge about language can increase the interest, understanding and pleasure of reading in many ways. Let us consider, for example, the reading of a text – Dickens's *Bleak House*. Any reader of *Bleak House* will be struck by the fact that the story is told by two narrators, one impersonal and anonymous, and the other the innocent heroine. The anonymous narrator works in the third person and in the present tense, creating a paradoxical mixture of immediacy and generalising continuity, whereas Esther Summerson's first person narrative tells the same events in the past tense as though they were finished and distant. The famous first paragraph was quoted to some members of the Committee by a primary school head who uses it as an example of how writers like Dickens may effectively break rules of discourse for particular ends – 'as long as they know the rules in the first place'. The novel begins: 'London. Michaelmas Term lately over, and the Lord Chancellor sitting in Lincoln's Inn Hall. Implacable November weather.' It proceeds in a series of verbless sentences to describe a kind of static eternity of fog, using present participles: 'creeping', 'hovering', 'drooping', 'looming', 'hanging' etc. The novel presents a contrast of the lassitude and torpidity of the law and the upper classes with the fierce energy of Dickens's good men. Both of these qualities are indicated with long strings of adjectives and adverbs. Mr Boythorn is 'an honourable, obstinate, truthful, high-spirited, intensely prejudiced, perfectly unreasonable man', remarkable, Esther says, 'in the very fury of his superlatives, which seemed to go off like blank cannons and hurt nothing'. On the other hand, the anonymous narrator describes Mr Tulkinghorn's garments: 'Mute, close, irresponsive to any glancing light, his dress is like himself.'

22.   In the following extract, describing the pauper's burial of a typhus victim, the use of antithesis and echoes from earlier biblical language give force to Dickens's indignation.

With houses looking on, on every side, save where a reeking little tunnel of a court gives access to the iron gate – with every villainy of life in action close on death, and every poisonous element of death in action close on life – here, they lower our dear brother down a foot or two: here, sow him in corruption, to be raised in corruption: an avenging ghost at many a sick-bedside: a shameful testimony to future ages, how civilisation and barbarism walked this boastful island together.

The punctuation, with its hurried dashes followed by deliberate colons, repays study; so does the organisation of the whole complex sentence.

23. Changes in language over time might well be exemplified by the changes in the passage from I Corinthians 15 which appears in the Anglican Burial Service and is parodied and adapted by Dickens's angry irony in the last quotation. Here are some different versions of that passage:

So is the resurreccyon of the dead. It is sowen in corrupcion, it ryseth again in incorrupcion. It is sowē in dishonour, it ryseth agayne in honour. It is sowen in weaknesse, it ryseth agayn in power. It is sowen a naturiall bodie, it ryseth agayn a spirituall bodie. There is a naturall bodie, and there is a spirituall bodye: as it is also written: The firste manne Adam was made liuing soule, and the last Adam was made a quickning spirite . . . The firste man is of the earthe, yearthy: The second manne is the Lorde from heauen (heauenly).
(From the First Prayer-Book of Edward VI, 1549)

So also is the resurrection of the dead. It is sown in corruption: it is raised in incorruption; it is sown in dishonour; it is raised in glory: it is sown in weakness; it is raised in power: it is sown a natural body; it is raised a spiritual body . . . And so it is written, The first man Adam was made a living soul; the last Adam was made a quickening spirit . . . The first man is of the earth, earthy: the second man is the Lord from heaven.
(From the Book of Common Prayer, 1662)

So it is with the resurrection of the dead. What is sown is perishable, what is raised is imperishable. It is sown in dishonour, it is raised in glory. It is sown in weakness, it is raised in power. It is sown a physical body, it is raised a spiritual body.
(From the Alternative Service Book (1950) using the Revised Standard Version)

So it is with the resurrection of the dead. What is sown in the earth as a perishable thing is raised imperishable. Sown in humiliation, it is raised in glory; sown in weakness, it is raised in power; sown as an animal body, it is raised as a spiritual body.

If there is such a thing as an animal body, there is also a spiritual body. It is in this sense that Scripture says, 'The first man, Adam, became an animate being', whereas the last Adam has become a life-giving spirit. The first man was made 'of the dust of the earth': the second man is from heaven.
(From the New English Bible, 1970)

A comparison of these texts shows the language in process of change, both in form and meaning. A student of language could find much that is fascinating about the variety of spellings in the earlier texts; it can be observed that the same word does not always consist of the same letters (*bodie, bodye*) and that sentence breaks are not marked by full stops. A discussion of the rhythm of the sentences is also interesting – the two more modern versions both try to make the antitheses briefer and more terse. The Revised Standard Version, which preserves some of the uncompromising rhythm of the Book of Common Prayer, is arguably much more successful.

24. Much may also be observed about the history of words and their changes of meaning. In the early versions the last Adam is described as 'a quickening spirit' using a near-obsolete meaning of 'quick' or 'quicken' which persists in 'the quick and the dead' or an occasional description of the child quickening in the womb. 'Life-giving' in the New English Bible is not a precise synonym. Other synonyms or near-synonyms are interesting. What is the difference between a 'natural' body, a 'physical' body and an 'animal' body? What is the difference between 'living soul' in Edward VI and 'animate being' in the New English Bible? This in turn raises the question of the Latin origins of *animated,* and the difference between 'living' and 'animate'. Tense and voice are also interesting: in Edward VI,

the body 'ryseth'; in Common Prayer it 'is raised', which suggests an agency raising it. And the texts can also be studied in terms of those parts of the model that relate to communication and interaction. If Edward VI moves rapidly forward in a state of convinced excitement, what are we to make of the appearance in the New English Bible of qualifying, or even questioning phrases not in earlier texts. 'If there is such a thing as . . .', 'It is in this sense that Scripture says . . .'. Compare this with the certainty of 'it is written . . .' in Edward VI. We might also notice that the association of corruption of the body, corruption in the state and the known rhythms of this text that Dickens relied on in his burial description are lost by the Revised Standard Version and New English Bible. How far is *corrupt* not a synonym for *perishable*? What are the connotations of each?

25. Knowledge of the structure of sentences and discourse can also be invaluable in making both form and meaning of earlier poetry accessible to young people. Donne's verse paragraphs have a colloquial forcefulness – 'For Godsake hold your tongue, and let me love.' They are all highly structured complex sentences whose meaning and emphasis can be revealed by the pinpointing of the main verb. This is also true of Milton's sonnet on his blindness 'When I consider how my light is spent . . .'. The octet consists of one sentence built of piled-up clauses and questionings; the main verb appears only as the third word of the eighth line 'I fondly ask'. The sestet consists of Patience's clear and not at all convoluted answer to the question. Again, finding the main verb both reveals the structure of the poem and clarifies the meaning.

26. An appreciation of poetry and prose, old and new, requires and influences a knowledge about language – its forms, variations, development and powers of concision. A look at one short verse from W. H. Auden's 'The Shield of Achilles' can show how an attention to the language can help a student towards an appreciation of the effect.

> A ragged urchin, aimless and alone,
>   Loitered about that vacancy, a bird
> Flew up to safety from his well-aimed stone:
>   That girls are raped, that two boys knife a third,
>   Were axioms to him, who'd never heard
> Of any world where promises were kept.
> Or one could weep because another wept.

The boy is 'aimless' but his stone is 'well-aimed' (because to throw a stone at a bird is aimless, in the sense of pointless) which suggests that it is a moral 'vacancy' that he inhabits as well as an actual one. The use of the conversational elision 'who'd', for the sake of rhythm, shows that poetry does not always have to have its best clothes on, and is closely allied to natural speech. To 'weep' because another 'wept' shows how grammatical forms can in themselves carry meaning. The form of 'wept' is that of the past tense, but when it is juxtaposed with that of the present tense 'weep' it provides a sense of the continuity of human feeling permanently in the present. The verse shows, too, the importance of rhyme for emotional effect, and memorableness. 'A boy who had never heard of any world where promises are kept, and that a person could weep because he saw that someone else was weeping' is not the same, although it means the same.

27. Prose of all kinds can be used to provide examples of the way language knowledge can inform and extend understanding of literature. The first pages of *Bleak House*, as we have shown, or *Portrait of the Artist*

as a Young Man, almost any page or George Eliot of V. S. Naipaul – all are rich mines for literacy and linguistic working. In literature, above all, students will experience the force of language, realise its power to stir, entertain and move.

28. There are many ways of absorbing this power. Very young children enjoy learning and reciting poetry. There is no reason why they should not continue to do so during the rest of their school years. To develop an ear for language, for rhythm and intonation, for feeding and stockpiling the memory, nothing can compare with learning poems by heart, so long as the poems are chosen by the pupils themselves. Poetry can be a lifelong pleasure which ideally teachers should want to share with their pupils, through poems they love, and poems children have themselves found in anthologies and elsewhere. As Octavio Paz says, 'every creative act begins as imitation and ends as invention'.

29. There are other powerful forces with which readers come into contact and which should be explored. Information surrounds pupils in schools – charts, diagrams, newspapers, television and, increasingly, databases and teletext. Information in such profusion can be daunting or confusing. One of the purposes of producing fluent young readers is to ensure that they gain access to the power such information can provide. It is important, moreover, that pupils are enabled to sift gist from incidentals, and fact from surmise or subterfuge. The language of newspapers, for example, and indeed of television and radio, merit attention in the classroom. Comparison of newspaper headlines and the recognition and clarification of ambiguity, or drawing parallels and differences between the same event reported in, say, *The Sun, The Independent* and *The Times* makes pupils realise that language can obscure truth as well as reveal it. It should profitably lead to a focus on the vocabulary and syntax which produces such manipulation.

Talking and listening
Attitudes to talk

30. People engaged in talking and listening are in a much more reciprocal relationship than that contracted by a writer and reader. Speech occurs for the most part as an event involving two or more people simultaneously. Generally, people listen in order to speak next or at a later point, and speak directly to listeners who, in a variety of ways, signal at the time of listening their interpretation and reception of what is said. Moreover, speech takes place, most of the time for most people, as a social event rather than as an informational, directive or artistic endeavour. There is also much more speech than writing. The majority of the many millions of words spoken constantly in homes, pubs, offices and streets manifests a form of social behaviour which operates under rules which are different from those governing writing. Classrooms, if they are to prepare children for adulthood, must reflect that behaviour.

31. Teachers may well display habits of speech which are different from those of their pupils' parents. The use of any accent should not pose a practical problem for teacher or child except when a localised English accent or one deriving from a first language other than English is adversely affecting easy and confident communication. It is important for teachers to have clear and informed views about accent. For example, it is indefensible to make a pupil feel at any time and in any way ashamed of his or her accent. As one witness to the Committee pointed out, 'More than 12 years ago, the Bullock Report declared fairly . . . ''We believe that a child's accent should be accepted, and that to attempt to suppress it is

irrational and neither humane nor necessary . . .".' The same witness went on to relate an incident observed in a classroom: 'Yet only recently I heard a tape recording of some 11-year-olds . . . in Northumberland who were being asked to tell the teacher about a book they had been looking at. One of them said – in the accent of the region – "It's aboot (about) tigers." His teacher said "Not a *boot*, Nigel; a boot is something you wear on your foot . . .".'

32. Uninformed attitudes to language are not confined to the feature of accent. This is not surprising, since language above all else is the defining characteristic of an individual, a community, a nation. It is understandable that people feel themselves to be proprietors of their own language, and that they should feel their ownership to be violated by the use of language different from their own. The relationship between personality or identification with a community and the common ownership of a language is so close that there is a tendency for people to feel that *their* language is the best. But facts are otherwise. All languages are rule-governed systems of communication, and none is linguistically superior.

33. It should be the duty of all teachers to instil in their pupils a civilised respect for other languages and an understanding of the relations between other languages and English. It should be made clear to English-speaking pupils that classmates whose first language is Bengali or Cantonese, or any other of the scores of languages spoken by the school population (over 160 in inner London alone) have languages quite as systematic and rule-governed as their own. Teachers should be helping children whose first language is not English to acquire accents in English which will enable them to be understood easily. They should also be helping children to acquire the vocabulary, syntax and conventions which are characteristic of different types of discourse. Informed and socially productive attitudes will flourish in classrooms where both children and teachers are accustomed to treat language as a fit subject for study. Pupils are most likely to acquire such attitudes and accompanying knowledge through active investigation.

Purposes of talk 34. In addition to encouraging the development of speech for communication, teachers need to encourage talk which can be exploratory, tentative, used for thinking through problems, for discussing assigned tasks, and for clarifying thought: talk is not merely social and communicative, it is also a tool for learning. To say 'merely' is not to dismiss talk that is intended as a performance. Often both kinds of talk emerge from the same activity. For example, children engaged in making a radio broadcast on tape will need to grapple with a series of questions before the broadcast is made. What should be the main story? How should the headlines be phrased? How much are the listeners likely to know already on this topic? How far is it a sensitive issue which needs to be handled with special tact – which ways of putting things will be more or less acceptable and why? What sort of voice is appropriate? What sort of vocabulary is best suited to the speaker and the audience? How best should question-sentences be constructed? How should one item be linked to items which follow and precede? In extending pupils' abilities to present an argument rationally and logically, there are different questions to be asked. How long should 'turns' of conversation be? What influence will the respective social roles of speakers and listeners have on choices of language used? How far is the force of an argument influenced by such extra-linguistic factors as physical gesture, stance and so on? Given help from teachers who have assimilated knowledge about language as outlined in the model of Chapter 3, pupils will be given opportunities to reflect upon differences in language which are determined by different contexts, audiences and purposes, and be able to do so. By devising different tasks for different purposes, teachers will enable pupils better to cope with the challenge of school across the whole curriculum, not only in English. In order to illustrate good practice, we present some examples of classroom activity.

Example i: 7-year-olds

35.   To a class of 7-year-old children, most of whom were born of Asian parents, a teacher read a fairy tale. The aim of the lesson was to stimulate an interest in the ways in which words are used to create meaning. The children were excited by the story, and after some discussion decided to produce a display in pictorial form. This they did, but when they came to put the pictures in order, they found that they needed to use words as well to convey the story. It was decided to use one word to describe each picture. The children decided that it would be helpful if they used the English word alongside the Urdu equivalent in each case. This decision gave rise to further discussion about the use of language, but particularly pronunciation. The word *clever* was used alongside a picture, and the children were encouraged to discover an equivalent word in Urdu. They decided that the closest to it was *hoshyar*. The teacher then learned from the children how it should be pronounced, and tried to discover if it was a literal translation. This discussion led on to a further enquiry about words that have similar meanings. Eventually, a list of these was written up in the classroom. The teacher then went on to discuss words that are opposite in meaning to 'clever', and the children produced a list of opposites in both English and Urdu. Here was a good example of children being brought to a point of learning where *reflection* on the nature and use of language was both natural and necessary. And this reflection is induced by teaching which is informed by knowledge about language.

Example ii: 11-year-olds

36.   In a class of 11-year-olds visited by the Committee, the pupils had been divided into groups of four to discuss whether the rights of individuals are threatened by establishing No Smoking areas in public places. One member of each group was elected to provide a summary of that group's discussion. The elected reporter gave a one-minute summary of his or her group's discussion, standing up in front of the class (with the lights at the front of the class being dipped 10 seconds before the minute was up). Each summary was then commented on by a member of another group, in terms of, for example:

- how clear the summary was
- whether the speaker kept repeating the same structure or vocabulary
- whether the speaker made the discussion appear interesting
- whether the speaker represented only one point of view or was able to represent several points of view
- whether the speaker stood up straight and looked at all members of the audience or kept looking just to one side of the class
- whether the speaker was fluent or paused too much
- whether the speaker was adequately audible at the back
- whether the speed of the speech was appropriate.

After each critique, other members of the class offered their observations, often including a critique of 'unjust' criticisms made by the previous speaker. This was clearly a familiar format and most pupils participated.

The tightly constrained format ensured a rapid progression of discussion so that a great deal of work was done in what seemed a very short time.

37. The teacher intervened rather little except to ensure that the opportunities for class comment were widely distributed throughout the class. He also made notes on problems of expression which some speakers had, asking them, when they had finished speaking, what they had been trying to say in using a particular expression and drawing the class into a discussion of why the expression chosen was unclear and how the thought that the pupil wished to express might be better formulated. Then he wrote on the board a range of suggestions from the class, considering which of these were improvements on the original and why. Children who are informed when what they say is unclear learn to express themselves clearly, whereas children whose unclear expression is ignored, or simply 'interpreted' by a sympathetic adult, lack the feedback which informs them when their expression is unclear, and so continue to express themselves in an unclear manner.

38. This teacher was aware that some members of the class found the format, which the other members gave every indication of enjoying, too stressful, so that their participation was minimal. He would encourage these less confident pupils to work in small groups, in less demanding ways. For example, they would report on a set of instructions rather than on the structure of an argument, or give an account of one side of an argument rather than attempt to give an account of opposing points of view. Rather than addressing the whole class, they would report only to the other members of the group, tape-recording their report so that members could play it back and co-operate in commenting on what was said, formulating together, where necessary, what the speaker was trying to express. The teacher explained that in his experience this work would lead to an increase of confidence among these pupils, which would eventually enable them to participate fully when the whole class was working together.

39. The teacher's understanding of the different demands of different communicative situations permitted him to identify a mode of proceeding in which the less confident pupils could make progress: his understanding of the characteristics of different types of discourse (most pupils cope better with narrative than with argument) permitted him to modify what these pupils were asked to do in such a way that they could be successful in the less demanding type, even if they were not yet ready to participate fully in the more demanding activity.

Listening 40. So far, our emphasis has been on talking, but listening should not be ignored. The Committee accepts that too often in the recent past so-called 'listening exercises' have been mechanistic drills with little relevance to the experience or interest of pupils. Listening is not a simple matter of hearing. Successful listeners adapt their *mode* of listening to their *intention* in listening: so they 'skim and sample' what is being said when the topic is of little interest to them but pay close attention, if necessary for some minutes at a time, when what is being said is important to them. One of the things which a successful listener has to learn is when it is important to listen carefully – just as a successful reader is able to identify when skimming is all that is required and when careful and patient rereading is necessary. The good listener actively interprets incoming information – not only information about the topic but also information about the speaker's beliefs, prejudices, apparent attitude to what is being said, and so on. The information has to be related to relevant background knowledge, as well as what has already been said in the discourse, and the listener has to construct a coherent interpretation, making sensible inferences to fill out what is actually said, and, if necessary, putting to use this information by answering a question, passing on a message, taking medicine, going to the bank, etc.

41.   Teachers can help pupils who have difficulty in listening carefully at appropriate times by identifying for them the occasion, when it is important for them to listen carefully and checking that they have done so. Teachers can also provide practice and support for pupils who, in a formal context where they are somewhat intimidated, tend to panic and to fail to relate what is said to what they already know.

Example i: 14-year-olds

42.   In the following example, a group of pupils is following a set of sound-taped instructions to draw a route on a town plan which they had in front of them.

[Tape: now go round to the left and stop in front of the National Monument.]
P : there isn't a National Monument – Miss, there isn't one – we can't do it
T : now think – what did we say that statue was?
P : a monument – to the war dead – oh that'll be the National Monument

43.   This example illustrates a common problem for weaker pupils – that there may be many different ways of making reference to the same object. A teacher who diagnoses this problem will usefully spend time exploring with the pupils the many different ways of referring to common objects and individuals well-known to them, and the contexts in which different expressions are likely to be used (e.g. *David, David Smith, Dave, Mrs Smith's son, the boy at the front of the class, the goalie, the trombone player, last year's swimming champion, the boy who's just been talking,* etc.)

44.   In monitoring pupils' ability to listen with attention and put to use what is heard, it is often helpful to draw their attention to exactly what was said and to demonstrate that what was said does not justify the extra inferences which they make.

Example ii: 15-year-olds

45.   In our second example, pupils are again being asked to follow instructions from a sound tape:

[Tape: now draw a line along the square]
P : has it to go – has it to go along the square – or half – just to the middle?
T : what did it say?
P : put a line along – just said 'along'
T : did it say to stop in the middle?
P : no – so it just goes along the length of the square!

46.   The teacher correctly identifies the pupil's unwarranted inference and draws attention to the fact that the utterance is not consistent with this extra inference. Less able pupils are particularly liable to make unconstrained interpretations: the teacher can play a valuable role in helping such pupils to listen carefully to precisely what was said and to draw only the minimally necessary inferences in circumstances where elaborate inferences are not required (as it might be, for instance, in the interpretation of a poem). A further valuable aid for weaker pupils can be to encourage them to listen so carefully that they notice, and ask about, inconsistencies in what they hear. It is well established that some children are 'hearer-blamers' – that is, if they hear an ambiguous or unclearly

formulated message, they will assume that it is *their* fault if they fail to understand it. Encouraging such pupils to identify what is unclear in the message and to question this (drawing attention to the ambiguous referring phrase or structure) can positively benefit pupils with this problem. This is a problem which many of us will share to some degree where the speaker is 'an expert' and we, as listeners, are in a 'non-expert' role.

Example iii: 14-year-olds

47.   In the following extracts from lessons, a small group of 14-year-old pupils is in each case playing a game where they hear instructions on a tape and they are supposed to challenge the tape if something is said which is not clear, in which case the teacher fills in the extra information which they require:

[Tape: then put a '6' inside the square that has a circle inside it]
P1 : there isn't a square with a circle in it
P2 : well we'll make one – where do we draw the circle?
P3 : no it might be just a mistake
P1 : right – we'd better check – Miss – should it be a circle in a square?
T : well done – no, it shouldn't be – what should it be?
P1 : they must have got it muddled – we've got a circle with a square in it – do they mean that?
T : absolutely right – well done

[Tape: now turn into Nations Road and go up to the pagoda]
P1 : here's the pagoda – but it's not in Nations Road
P2 : that's called the Heaven's Gate Pagoda – ours is just 'pagoda'
P3 : could be the same pagoda
P4 : there's another pagoda along here – called the White Cloud Pagoda that's just off Nations Road
P1 : so it must be there
P4 : better check – Miss – when you're at Nations Road do you turn left or right to go up to the pagoda?
T : it wasn't clear was it? – you should turn right
P4 : so it is the White Cloud Pagoda?
T : yes – that's right
P2 : how come it's not named then?
T : that was ambiguous too – they just said 'pagoda' which could apply to either of them – but it's clear once you've turned to the right

48.   The teacher will see that P2 has problems in both these extracts: in the 'square and circle' example, P2 is ready to draw in an extra part of the diagram – the others, more cautious and having learned from playing this game before, try to restrict the interpretation and identify the point that needs to be checked. In the 'pagoda' example, P2 is misled by the fact that the tape uses a general expression ('the pagoda') to refer to what she sees on the plan with a specific name. Once the teacher has identified this pupil's problems, more specific help of the kind illustrated here can be provided.

49.   Quite apart from learning to listen to what is being said, learning to interpret and, where appropriate, to put interpretation to use, pupils may also be helped to listen to the *form* of what is said – to hear which words rhyme in their own and others' speech, and in poems they are studying, to hear the effects of assonance, alliteration, end-lines, caesuras and how many syllables there are in a line. They can be helped to identify where the emphasis lies in an utterance, what sort of 'tone of voice' is used, hence what sort of attitude speakers express using different 'tones of voice'. All of this is valuable in reading poetry and in role-play and play-reading.

Co-ordinating language study in schools

50.   In many schools in England, 'language awareness courses' of different kinds are being taught. These courses vary in quality. In some schools which offer language awareness courses, we have met an enthusiastic openness to language study which we applaud. It can only be sensible for all teachers of language in a school – whether they are teaching French or Latin, English or Punjabi – to ensure that they are using the same framework of description for talking about language and employing the same descriptive vocabulary. It can only be sensible to make overt comparisons between languages which the pupils know, so that they can be led to see the general principles of language structure and use, through a coherent and consistent approach.

51.   However, some of the materials which have been developed, ostensibly in line with this approach, offer only a superficial and unsystematic description of some aspects of language phenomena which can each be treated briefly in a single period. Of much greater value, we believe, is the co-ordination of all language teaching within a school in the way we have described. There can be little doubt that a school which has developed such a co-ordinated language teaching policy will also offer support for the teaching of English, in particular teaching knowledge about English language. Such a policy will be of value to teachers both of English and of foreign languages, as well as to those dealing with the language used in the teaching of other subjects. Accordingly,

The Committee recommends that all subject departments concerned with the teaching of language in secondary schools (including English – whether as a first or second language – and foreign languages, ancient or modern) develop a co-ordinated policy for language teaching.

52.   In the Bullock Report, principal recommendation no. 5 asked for the presence of a 'language consultant' in every primary school. Many schools now have members of staff designated as language consultants, but certainly not every school. The Committee believes that every primary school should have at least one appropriately qualified member of staff to act as a co-ordinator of language work. Accordingly,

The Committee recommends that all primary schools should have a member of staff who is designated as a language consultant, and who has the responsibility for advising on and co-ordinating language work, including knowledge about language.

Time for language

53.   'Knowledge about language' is not a separate component of the primary or secondary curriculum. It should not be 'bolted on', but should inform children's talking, writing, reading and listening in the classroom. Some aspects of this report will require language consultants in primary schools and heads of English in secondary schools to review existing practice and perhaps incorporate new elements into the curriculum. It is clear that the time required for English on the secondary school timetable will need to be sufficient to ensure that pupils enjoy a curriculum which provides them with the opportunities and experiences to achieve, so far as possible, the attainment targets set out in Chapter 5.

The Committee recommends that the Secretary of State ensure that all schools should review existing provision for English to secure sufficient curriculum time to implement the findings of this report.

Chapter 5 *Entitlement, attainment and assessment*

Curricular entitlement

1. The Committee's view that language is central to education is clear from the foregoing chapters. That view is derived from our recognition of the importance of language in adult life and from the fact that children's intellectual development, hence their progress in most aspects of the school curriculum, depends upon an ability to use and understand language. There is no need to justify the claim that all children in school are entitled to be helped to achieve the highest possible levels of linguistic competence and understanding, but there is a need to say what that competence and understanding should be.

2. We have stated in general terms the kind of competence and understanding which we take to be the right of all pupils in the education system. How they gain access to that right will depend on what provision is made for them in school, and on how teachers use their knowledge about language in order to provide appropriate experiences for their pupils. The Committee endorses the statement in the Report of the Task Group on Assessment and Testing (TGAT):

A school can function effectively only if it has adopted:
– clear aims and objectives;
– ways of gauging the achievement of these;
– comprehensible language for communicating the extent of those achievements to pupils, their parents and teachers, and to the wider community, so that everyone involved can take informed decisions about future action.
(Chapter 1 paragraph 2)

What applies to a school applies equally to subject departments, and to individual teachers in both primary and secondary schools. There must be general aims and there must be a series of specific objectives to achieve those aims. The objectives for the language aims of Chapter 2 can be described in terms of attainment targets for different age-groups.

3. We regard it as the entitlement of all pupils to be enabled to achieve as far as they can the attainment targets proposed in this chapter. It will be the responsibility of schools, departments and individual teachers to decide precisely how to help them reach the targets, in terms of specific classroom activities. But the notion of entitlement implies that these targets, and appropriate programmes of study leading up to them, should be incorporated in the national curriculum.

Attainment targets

4. We have argued that education must encourage the growth and development of each individual's intellectual capacities and to prepare the child to enter adult life, as fully informed as possible about the nature of society, as capable as possible of making informed choices, and of contributing to the well-being of the community. Throughout this report, this is implied and is the chief reason why we present attainment targets for knowledge about language in the order given, starting with the objectives for age 16.

5.   The lists of targets reflect ordered sets of criteria. First, there are criteria determined by the social purposes of education, and by the needs for personal development insofar as these are concerned with knowledge about language. These also involve preparation for entry to further or higher education, for employment, and for the bringing up of children. Next, there are criteria determined by the model of language. And third, consideration has been given to how success in attaining the targets will be gauged. The ordering of the attainment targets does not reflect a view of their relative importance but follows that of the presentation of the model.

6.   There are two further considerations. The first is concerned with what is meant by *knowledge*, for there are different kinds of knowledge. There is the kind of knowledge which people acquire and can act upon, without necessarily being able or needing to explain it: this is 'knowing *how*'. It is what we might call 'implicit' knowledge, as distinct from the kind of knowledge which is analytical, definable, or 'explicit' – knowledge in the sense of 'knowing *about*'. Both are necessary. The second consideration is about the ways in which both kinds of knowledge relate to teaching aims and objectives. We have considered in some detail the opportunities and the practical tasks that are likely to arise, the skills that are required and the knowledge about language which will assist in acquiring such skills.

7.   Our targets (see p. 52) are set out in parallel columns: on the left are those relating to the acquisition of *implicit* knowledge which define a set of competences underlying the effective use of English. On the right are those relating to *explicit* knowledge; each is numbered, and the left- and right-hand numbers correlate.

8.   Throughout the lists which follow, the word *understand* frequently appears in the right-hand columns. We have chosen this term to refer to the second kind of knowledge mentioned above – the *explicit* knowledge. The term *understand* has been chosen, rather than *explain*, or *define*, because we have throughout had in mind the necessary variety of good teaching practice in schools. Teachers must decide how to gauge the levels of pupils' understanding, and they will use different methods: some may ask for direct explanations, others may judge pupils' understanding by less direct methods, such as assessing the quality of a critique or commentary.

9.   Not all elements of any set of criteria need to apply to all targets. Nor need any element apply equally to talking, listening, reading and writing. As in the model itself, no one aspect is sufficient, but all are necessary. This reinforces the need for the aims of Chapter 2, the model in Chapter 3, the principles of application in Chapter 4 and the attainment targets now presented all to be regarded as interdependent, as of course are the targets themselves. Attainment targets are presented discretely, but reflect activities which are all interrelated in very complex ways. Both assessment procedures and classroom activities should respect that fact. The planning of both should acknowledge that different pupils develop different skills at different rates.

10.   Attainment must be measured in relation to meaningful tasks, not to operations performed on decontextualised bits of language. The achievement of *implicit* knowledge targets in the left-hand columns will be revealed in aspects of pupils' performance, however measured. The

achievement of *explicit* knowledge targets in the right-hand columns will be revealed by the extent to which pupils can rationalise and reflect upon their performance.

The Committee believes that it should be the entitlement of all pupils to be given the opportunity to attain the following targets.

The left-hand columns reflect aspects of pupil performance. The right-hand columns reflect aspects of language upon which pupils should be expected to reflect and comment in the light of knowledge about language.

Attainment targets at age 16

1. Speak in Standard English, using their own accents (provided that those accents do not impair comprehension by other speakers of English).

1. Understand how tone of voice, stress and intonation contribute to meaning in spoken English.

2. Read aloud with appropriate stress, intonation and pause.

2. Understand how elements of meaning are structured in a text and the relationships between features of speech and the content of the text – hence, how for example parentheses are marked off in speech from main utterances, or how matter already referred to or understood is marked off from new matter.

3. Use punctuation according to the conventions of Standard English.

3. Understand the functions of punctuation in Standard English.

4. Spell correctly.

4. Understand the relationships between sounds and spelling patterns, and related word patterns.

5. Use a wide and varied vocabulary according to different purposes and situations, in speech and in writing, and, as an aid to that end, be able to use dictionaries which give more information than simple spelling dictionaries.

5. Understand the main patterns of word formation displayed in English: this involves knowing about the forms of words used in public, academic, scientific, generally learned vocabularies (derived chiefly from Greek and Latin) as well as about the forms of everyday commonly used words and their derivations.

6. Use (in speech and writing) and appreciate (in reading and listening) a variety of syntactic structures including structures of complex sentences appropriate to purpose and situation.

6. Understand the syntax of phrases and sentences in Standard English, including that of complex sentences, and how the grammar of complex sentences relates to complex temporal, spatial, causal and intentional relationships.

7. Comprehend and create sustained texts of different kinds.

7. Understand the main linguistic devices by which coherence is achieved in a text.

8. Write legibly and easily.

8. Understand the different uses of different forms of handwriting: cursive, print, capitals.

9. Use, in speech and in writing, varieties of language which appropriately express different degrees of formality and informality.

9a. Understand the differences and relationships between speech and writing.

9b. Understand how different determinants of context, e.g. place, time, topic, attitude, affect language use.

9c. Have a simple knowledge of the stages in the individual's acquisition and development of language from birth to adulthood.

10. Express feelings and intentions as well as facts, ideas and arguments lucidly, in speech and in writing.

10. Understand how language forms relate to different genres of language, e.g. narrative, argument, persuasion.

11. Be able to improve written work by re-writing.

11. Understand some of the ways in which the influence of written language on a reader is effected.

12. —

12. Understand that English, like all languages, is subject to change, and have some knowledge of the history of the English language as well as of current changes, with an appreciation of language change in relation to past as well as contemporary literature.

13. Make some systematic comparisons with other languages learned or used in school and in present day British society, so that an interest in linguistic diversity might be encouraged.

13. Understand that
- all languages are rule-governed systems
- the status accorded to different languages used in any community is determined by social rather than linguistic factors.

14. Use accurate if simple technical description in discussing language and the effects of language, and apply such description to speech forms as well as to writing. Written language discussed should include a variety of non-fiction, fictional prose, drama and poetry.

Attainment targets at age 11

1. Read aloud, showing by use of intonation that they understand what is being read.

1. Understand how the main intonation patterns of English correspond to sentence and phrase boundaries (e.g. full stops and commas).

2. Use capital letters and the main punctuation devices of English (full stop, comma, question mark and quotation marks) as well as marking of paragraphs and dialogue.

2. Understand the functions of the main punctuation devices of English.

3. Use common derived word-forms (differing forms of same word-stem) and search for appropriate stem forms in a dictionary (e.g. *buy*, not *bought*).

4. Write using complete sentence forms correctly and appropriately and be able to identify omission or incorrect use in their own and others' work.

5. Use complex sentences appropriately to express complex relationships.

6. Write in well-organised paragraphs.

7. Write clearly enough to enable a reader to understand what is being referred to, either elsewhere in the text or in the outside world.

8. Be able to improve written work by re-writing.

9. Write legibly.

3. Understand common lexical derivation patterns of English words.

4a. Understand the difference between the main simple sentence patterns of English (statement, question, etc.) and the various ways in which different forms can be used.

4b. Understand that a complete sentence requires a main verb, and the part which the main verb plays in a sentence.

4c. Understand that, in general, statements require a subject noun phrase, and the part which the subject noun phrase plays in the sentence.

4d. Understand the ways in which adjectives and adverbs can be used to make 'referring expressions' clearer, and to improve description.

5. Understand that different relationships may be expressed by sequences of simple sentences, simple co-ordinated sentences, and complex sentences containing subordinate clauses.

6. Understand the conventions of paragraphing, e.g. indentation for the start of a paragraph or for dialogue attributed to new speakers.

7. Understand how a text is made coherent by clear 'referring expressions', consistent use of tenses, consistent style (e.g. in choice of vocabulary), as well as by conjunctions and punctuation which mark the relationship between what is said now with what has been said already, and what is to follow.

8. Understand some of the ways in which writing can be improved for defined purposes.

9. Understand the different uses of cursive and printed forms of writing.

10. Spell correctly.

10. Understand the main relationships between vowel and consonant sounds and the spelling regularities of English.

11. Be able to infer meanings which are left inexplicit in the text.

11. Understand how the contexts in which writing is produced lead to constraints on the expression of meanings which differ from those applying to speech.

12. Recognise from what they read and hear that language can be used persuasively.

12. Understand how presentational and rhetorical devices can be used for different purposes.

13. Make a brief but systematic observation of some of the ways in which dialect forms differ from those of Standard English.

13a. Understand that local forms and dialect forms may be appropriate in some contexts, e.g. when writing dialogue, but that for most of the time written English requires the use of Standard English.

13b. Understand that people who use English as a second language already use a fully developed first language.

13c. Understand that English is a world language
- as a first language (and where)
- as a second language (and where)
- as a foreign language

14. Talk and listen, both in groups and in a whole class, in a variety of forms: narrating, explaining, justifying, describing situations and feelings, giving instructions and conveying information, playing a role, putting forward and countering an argument.

14. —

15. Use and understand such terms of description as are necessary when discussing their language with teachers.

Attainment targets at age 7

1. Read passages of simple sentences (aloud as well as silently) with understanding.

1. Understand main correspondences between letters and speech-sounds and know the alphabet.

2. Listen with comprehension to spoken language.

2. —

3. Write simple sentences, using full stops, capital letters and commas, word spacing and appropriate word forms.

3. Understand sentence boundaries, i.e. what a full stop and a capital letter are for.

4. Be able to vary sentence length where appropriate.

4. Understand that simple sentences obey rules of word-order.

5. Spell common words correctly.

5. Understand that spelling obeys rules.

6. Be able to redraft writing.

6. Understand that writing can be improved for known purposes.

7. Be able to articulate clearly, and express well what is intended.

7. Understand that a listener must be able to hear what is said, and understand what is meant.

8. Use legible handwriting.

8. —

9. —

9. Understand that non-verbal features contribute to oral communication and that degrees of formality and informality matter.

10. Write in a variety of forms, namely: story, poem, or comments on investigations, expression of feelings, instructions or directions, narrative accounts of experience, simple explanations.

10. —

11. Talk and listen, in both group-work and in a whole class, in a variety of forms: telling and listening to stories, explaining, following/giving instructions, imaginative, collaborative play/learning, including problem-solving, asking/answering questions, sharing experiences.

11. Understand that talk is a normal, natural, necessary part of classroom life and one to which they should contribute.

12.- —

12.- Understand some of the ways in which people talk differently from one another.

13.- —

13.- Understand some of the ways in which talk and writing are different.

14.- Use and understand such simple terms of description as are necessary when discussing their language with teachers.

The Committee recommends that the attainment targets required by the third term of reference be those set out in this report.

Assessment
11. The Committee's terms of reference antedated the more detailed framework of criterion-referenced attainment targets, subject profiles and assessment arrangements proposed in the TGAT Report. We have however taken it into account in devising our targets. We envisage that the attainment targets covering knowledge about language will form part of the set of 'profile components' for English as a whole, to be drawn up by the Secretary of State's working group on English in the national curriculum.

The Committee recommends that the English working group should draw upon its proposed attainment targets in formulating profile components for the assessment of English in the national curriculum.

12.   TGAT stresses in its report that differentiation, progression and aggregation for reporting should be key features of the different subject working groups' work on assessment. Account also needs to be taken of the ten levels of attainment suggested in the TGAT Report. We believe that our proposals are consistent with TGAT's requirements. The Committee, however, wishes to make the following points in relation to those issues:

- we believe that high expectations motivate pupils
- wherever possible, pupils should be enabled to demonstrate positive achievement
- what is assessed should be, wherever possible, embedded in the normal work of the classroom. Pupils should be able to redraft written work for assessment
- we recognise the 'task-specific' nature of assessment – the notion that crucial features of language use relate to the specific situation and the precise task undertaken in whatever subject and that one cannot infer that a different task will produce the same kind of response or achievement
- 'testing' needs to be defined as broadly as possible. Pupils should be able to demonstrate what they can do with language in a wide variety of tasks and situations. This implies that teachers of all subjects need to record achievement in many different situations over a long period of time. Pupils' record cards, for example, can usefully be accompanied with evidence of their writing, with notes on the context and circumstances in which the pieces were written
- self-reporting and self-assessment are valuable ways of improving standards and increasing pupils' ability to reflect upon performance.

13.   Almost all of the evidence submitted to the Committee mentioned assessment, and expressed varied doubts about either the feasibility or the desirability of testing children, particularly at age 7. We share TGAT's view, however, that assessment at age 7 is essential in determining whether or not pupils are making adequate progress in the important early years of schooling. Teachers need to be able to identify where pupils need help. At age 7 it is not too early: deferred, it may be too late.

14.   One issue, frequently mentioned in the evidence, is the so-called 'backwash effect' of testing. It is feared that schools may narrow the experience of pupils, confining teaching only to what can be tested and the forms of the prevalent tests. There is some danger here: the widespread use of the comprehension exercise in English lessons derives from comprehension testing which is of long standing in public examinations – it is too narrow an approach to the development of skill in reading. Worse has been the multiple choice test of comprehension (when notionally 'right' answers are selected from given alternatives): *inter alia* this cannot take account of the subtleties of literary language or response. To produce or to use text books based on such approaches would be to ignore the spirit of our recommendations.

15.   If assessment procedures are sufficiently flexible, and take account of accepted good practice, they can provide positive guidelines for teachers, rather than a set of constraints. Teachers already have useful initiatives upon which to draw: GCSE coursework assessment, Pupil Profiling and Records of Achievement, as well as those primary classrooms where the monitoring of pupils' language development is

regarded as a complex process best undertaken not by simple tests that focus on small aspects of learning, in the hope that they illuminate the broad span of language learning, but by a systematic policy for formative assessment which benefits the learner, as well as providing useful information for parents. The form of assessment is very important: it can help to highlight key areas for development, or exaggerate less significant issues. The most useful kind of assessment is that which enables the teacher to look back over the child's language experience and identify the reasons for weakness in important areas, and which at the same time points to specific remedies.

16.   Two questions frequently raised in the evidence are the ability range at any age and the fact that there are children in schools who do not have English as a first language. Given a wide range of ability, it is very difficult to set tests to a specific year group in schools which will allow all pupils to do justice to themselves. Allied to that concern is the age-spread to be found in any school 'year' of pupils. Difficulties are compounded by the greater maturity, both physical and mental, of girls in relation to boys, between the ages of about 10 and 14. The Committee believes, however, that the framework devised by TGAT will adequately allow for desirable measures of differentiation.

17.   Our report is primarily concerned with children who speak English as a mother-tongue. Children in our schools who are speakers of languages other than English, including Afro-Caribbean creole languages, share the entitlement which we have defined, and should be given every possible opportunity to function effectively in an English-speaking society. It is not within our terms of reference to consider English as a Second Language (ESL) provision in detail, but we urge close co-operation between ESL specialists and teachers who are implementing our recommendations in primary and secondary schools.

18.   The Committee accepts the different kinds of assessment proposed by TGAT. First, there is the individual, 'diagnostic' assessment which is integral to all good teaching. The teacher's experience, knowledge and perception demand a continuing evaluation of each pupil's progress; it may be a matter of weekly, daily, hourly, even minute-by-minute judgements as to how well a pupil has understood, learned from, or otherwise responded to a task. Such assessment is informal and often impressionistic and intuitive, and none the worse for that *if impressions and intuitions are well-informed*. If, as the Committee asserts, pupils have a curricular entitlement to the kind of knowledge discussed earlier, they have an equal entitlement to the kind of assessment discussed here. Then there is the kind of institutional assessment developed by a school or a subject department. This may take the form of periodic assessments of pupils' progress in accordance with a policy devised by the department or school – sometimes agreed by a group of schools in the same locality, if they have similar intakes and philosophies. There is also the kind of national system such as that devised by the public examination boards for pupils of about 16, and now to be extended to all age-groups.

19.   In respect of knowledge about language, the Committee wishes to make a further recommendation. Since we are anxious to avoid the problems of 'backwash' which we have referred to, we propose that the attainment targets which become the subject of national testing techniques should be drawn largely from the left-hand columns of the targets as we set them out. The assessment of those targets in the

right-hand columns should for the most part be the responsibility of individual teachers and institutions. Accordingly

The Committee recommends that appropriate national testing techniques be applied to language in use and that assessment of explicit knowledge about language be largely the province of individual teachers and institutions, both kinds of assessment being necessary. These principles should be reflected in the respective arrangements for coursework assessment and written examinations in the GCSE.

Chapter 6   *The education and training of teachers*

1. This chapter is concerned largely with the education and training of secondary teachers of English and primary school language consultants. It is estimated that in 1995 there will be a demand for about 20,000 teachers of English in secondary schools in England. Of those, more than two-thirds are already in schools at the time this report is being written. It is clear then that both providers of in-service training and those who prepare students to enter teaching have heavy responsibilities. All colleges and institutes of education, polytechnics and university departments of education need to ensure that they are capable of equipping future teachers with the requisite knowledge and classroom strategies. And the onus on providers of in-service training is even greater. The Committee sees teacher-training, and especially in-service training, as constituting the chief element in whatever may result from this report.

Pre-service training (PST)

2. There are six routes which may be followed by those wishing to teach as English specialists in secondary schools and as language consultants in primary schools.
    i.   Students may take a Bachelor of Education degree (BEd) with English as a main subject. Only a small number of such degree courses have a modern English language component. Some (recently qualified) students may have followed a professional 'methodology' course intended to provide them with the qualifications necessary to become a 'language consultant' in primary schools. They will have completed a course according to the criteria laid down by the Secretary of State and operated by the Council for the Accreditation of Teacher Education (CATE) which includes 100 hours of a language course (but see below paragraph 5).
    ii. Students may take a BEd degree in Combined Studies including English, and a professional course of the kind mentioned at (i) above.
    iii. Students may take a BEd degree with a subject other than English, and a professional course of the kind mentioned at (i) above.
    iv. Students may take a Bachelor of Arts degree (BA) in English (a small number of such degrees contain a component related to the study of modern English language). These students will also need to take a Post-Graduate Certificate of Education (PGCE) course related to the teaching of English.
    v.   Students may take a combined subjects degree including English. These students will also need to take a PGCE as mentioned at (iv) above.
    vi. Students may take a degree in a subject or subjects other than English, with the PGCE requirements as mentioned at (iv) above.

3. Secondary teachers of English with *no* qualifications in English beyond GCE O-level or its equivalent include
    i.   graduates in other subjects (e.g. history, sociology, etc.) who, either by reason of their own interest in the subject, or through INSET experience, find themselves members of English departments
    ii. teachers who simply fill slots in an incomplete timetable, regardless of their specialist qualifications or experience. Thus, it may be that two or three teaching groups out of 28 teaching groups in a school may be

allotted to any teacher who happens not to be timetabled for his or her own subject when those two or three groups are timetabled for English

iii. those teachers who have no formal teaching qualifications whatsoever, beyond their experience in schools, which may have started with employment as 'instructors', drafted into a school staff from commerce or industry. They are relatively few in number

iv. those teachers who function chiefly as 'support staff', mainly in inner urban areas such as London, Birmingham or Bradford, where there are substantial numbers of bilingual pupils. Such teachers may themselves be bilingual, and graduates (or otherwise qualified teachers) from foreign countries, institutions or backgrounds, and whose linguistic or cultural experience is helpful in the teaching of pupils whose first language is not English.

4. According to the most up-to-date statistics available, 28 per cent of the total number of teachers of English in secondary schools have no discernible qualification beyond GCE O-level English, and they carry out 15 per cent of the total amount of English taught in secondary schools. For this reason alone (and there are many others), it is plain that in-service education and training has a most important part to play in the professional improvement of the teaching force.

5. It may appear, from the above, that intending primary phase teachers in training on a BEd course are better equipped with knowledge about the English language than intending secondary phase English specialists on a PGCE course. This is not necessarily true. Although a minimum of 100 hours for primary teachers is to be spent on 'the study of teaching language', that study 'may be through a combination of taught time, structured school experience, and private study' (DES Circular 3/84 paragraph 9). Some courses offer only 20 hours of 'taught time', others over 60. This latitude allows such variation in the amount and quality of tuition provided that the end is subverted. Therefore

The Committee recommends that all intending teachers of primary school children should undertake a language course in which the larger part of the time allocated to the course (i.e. over 50 per cent) be spent in direct tuition of knowledge about language as outlined in the model proposed in this report which is relevant to the primary school child as displayed through the attainment targets.

6. For secondary specialists in English, the PST route is via a first degree (in either English literature, English studies – however defined by the degree-awarding body – or a combined studies degree in which English is a component) followed by a one-year PGCE course. The Committee recognises the constraints on time available for tuition in English language within the time-scale outlined in a one-year course of which 15 weeks are taken up by teaching practice in schools. Nonetheless, and in full appreciation of the fact that any PGCE course cannot provide more than 20–24 weeks' tuition, intended to cover all aspects of training, the Committee's view is that all intending teachers of English in secondary schools should undertake a course which enables them to acquire, understand and make use of those elements of language study described in the model of language presented in this report. The emphases in such a course may differ from those in a course for primary phase teachers. For example, more emphasis may be put on the structure and functions of discourse types and rhetoric than on acquisition and development of language in the early years. More co-operation could take place between

subject specialist departments of teacher training establishments. There is, for example, merit in the suggestion that students of English and of modern languages should, where possible, work together in planning and delivering a 'language-focussed' project to a shared class of pupils. But however structured, there should be a compulsory language course. Therefore

The Committee recommends that all intending teachers of English in secondary schools should undertake a course which enables them to acquire, understand and make use of knowledge about language as outlined in the model proposed in this report which is relevant to the secondary school pupil as displayed through the attainment targets.

7. It is simplistic to assess the value of any course in terms solely of contact hours, the length of modular elements or other purely quantitative measures. Of much greater importance is the *quality* of training afforded, measured in terms of how well teachers in training have assimilated and can apply the knowledge, concepts, skills and techniques necessary for proficient teaching of their subject. That implies that while it is important that tuition be given, in the sense that knowledge be transmitted by their tutors, such knowledge is of little use unless it be related to classroom tasks and techniques. The *application* of knowledge should form a substantial component of all courses in pre-service education. There are various ways of ensuring this. Certainly, tasks assigned during periods of school practice should be demonstrably linked to college-based tuition. Students should be encouraged to reflect upon those aspects of language which they have taught in schools, so that they are able to conceptualise and justify their reasons for having taught them. Moreover, since notions of applicability vary according to subjective criteria, moderators should be appointed to check the standards of courses in all institutions or consortia of institutions.

The Committee recommends that all teacher training courses, all of which should contain a substantial component of tuition in language study, should be evaluated at regular intervals by external assessors or moderators who have both pedagogic and linguistic expertise.

8. It is desirable for *all teachers, of whatever phase or subject*, to have a coherent, if short, course in language. But the Committee recognises the many difficulties involved. For example, a physics teacher will (normally) have taken a first degree in physics, not by its nature designed to serve teaching needs. The teacher will also have taken a PGCE course to acquire the basic skills of classroom practice as applied to physics teaching. Teaching children of any age is a complex and demanding job and it is unrealistic to ask that a further element be included in an already-too-brief 20-week curriculum. This is not to dismiss the importance of 'Language across the curriculum', a topic emphasised to the teaching world by the Bullock Report. Although the notion of 'Language across the curriculum' was widely misinterpreted in the years after Bullock (see *Bullock Revisited*), it remains an important notion, but, given the time constraints on the PGCE, one which has to be addressed in detail in in-service education and training rather than pre-service training, if we are speaking of secondary specialists in subjects other than English. Nonetheless, the Committee believes that *all* intending secondary phase teachers of subjects other than English should have a short, coherent course in language study in pre-service training.

The Committee recommends that all intending secondary teachers of subjects other than English should satisfactorily complete a course

on knowledge about language based on the model presented in this report relevant to their specialist subjects in pre-service training.

9. Since such courses will necessarily be brief, and since their aim will be to affect classroom practice, it is also important that the practical applications of the course content should be clear. The PGCE will inevitably and rightly concentrate on subject-specific matters: the study of English language in relation to the specialist language should be continued in the probationary year of teaching. Therefore

The Committee recommends that all teachers in all subjects in all secondary schools should, as part of the requirements of their probationary year, be required to be engaged in some aspect of language study as it relates to their own specialist fields or subjects.

10. If these recommendations are to be implemented, then university departments of education, polytechnics and colleges must re-design their courses. In 1975, the Bullock Report asked for a compulsory course in language for all students in pre-service training. That requirement was not fulfilled except by a few colleges of education. We are now making a sharper request.

The Committee recommends that all providers of pre-service training for the teaching profession re-design their courses for intending teachers to meet the requirements of the relevant recommendations in this report.

11. The brevity of the PGCE has been mentioned several times. Since in this country first degrees in the humanities are not vocational degrees, there is no reason why a first degree in English should include among its topics 'children's language development' or 'dialect/Standard English variations'. There are still degrees in English literature in which the only formal aspects of language study are historical, in Old or Middle English. There are for several reasons fewer such degrees than existed a generation ago, and some recently established degrees in English do contain elements of language study. While no one doubts the value to an English teacher of a wide knowledge of English literature, that is not of itself a sufficient qualification for an English specialist in a secondary school. It is important to recognise that the teaching of English is as specialised and demanding as, say, the teaching of physics or mathematics. The evidence submitted to the Committee and its own observations show that most specialist English teachers have not undertaken study which fits the recommendations of this report. This is as much the concern of those who plan first degrees in English as it is of university departments of education. It is the Committee's view that by the end of this century, English specialists entering the profession as primary or secondary teachers should hold qualifications which clearly fit them for their work. This might well continue to mean a first degree in English or, perhaps, a BEd course with English as a main subject. All such courses should include sufficient study of contemporary linguistic form and function to ensure that such knowledge helpfully informs their work as teachers of English. This is not to deny access in exceptional circumstances to new entrants from English or other disciplines who have not followed such courses, but the Committee's view is that such new entrants will require appropriate in-service training. Accordingly

The Committee recommends that before the end of the century a prerequisite for entry to the teaching profession as an English specialist should normally be a first degree in English which

incorporates a study of both contemporary and historical linguistic form and use.

In-service education and training (INSET)

12.   There are considerable difficulties involved in providing INSET for English – a lack of money, time and people. Concerning lack of funding – evidence available to the Committee shows great disparity in provision offered by different local education authorities (LEAs). It is certainly true that several university-provided long courses in linguistics or language in education – for example courses leading to a master's degree – have failed to recruit sufficient numbers because teachers have not been able to secure secondment. With regard to time available, much depends upon the availability of temporary teachers to cover for those engaged in INSET; much depends upon the availability of LEA advisers, who are, in the main, the organisers of INSET. Individual schools find great difficulty in allowing staff adequate time for development, and the smaller the school staff the more difficult it is. We know, too, that competing demands for INSET time make it very difficult to add yet another subject for attention to tightly constrained programmes. Nonetheless, and despite these difficulties

The Committee recommends that English generally and knowledge about language in particular be included in the list of national priority areas under the Local Education Authority Training Grants Scheme with effect from the earliest possible date.

13.   The identification of English as an area of national priority means that approved LEA expenditure on in-service training for English would, under present rules, attract 70 per cent grant support from the Government. This would encourage training which would not otherwise take place if it fell within the local priority area at a lower percentage grant rate or was unsupported by specific central grant. We recognise that this would make a substantial inroad into the expenditure provision for the Training Grants Scheme (£207 million for 1988–89, of which £77 million relates to areas of national priority). Therefore

The Committee recommends that the Government review the scale of provision for the Training Grants Scheme so that adequate allowance is provided for English as long as the need exists and without putting necessary in-service training in other key areas at risk.

14.   Lack of expertise presents even greater problems. At present, people who are professionally expert in knowledge about language are spread over universities, polytechnics and colleges, but not necessarily involved in teacher-training. There is no readily available agency to co-ordinate that expertise. Therefore, the Committee believes that only a nationally devised, administered and funded scheme could remedy the lack of expertise. The Department of Education and Science, with the help of H M Inspectorate, should, in the Committee's view, *first* – arrange for the identification of people with relevant expertise, either directly recruited or seconded, drawing upon both those few training institutions and those university departments where the linguistic expertise *does* exist; and *second* – arrange for their deployment through the country, with the responsibility of providing training for selected staff, who in turn would have the responsibility for training other teachers. That responsibility should include the fostering of initiatives akin to those generated by the National Writing Project, and the inclusion in such an enterprise of 'distance learning' – a technique successfully used by the Open University. Some such pattern of training is necessary if INSET is to be

taken seriously, since teachers' long courses (one term or more) in language study are diminishing through lack of secondment funding by LEAs. Accordingly

The Committee recommends that a nationally devised, administered and funded scheme should arrange for people with relevant expertise to provide training both for selected staff in institutions where relevant expertise does not exist, and for selected staff in schools, such training to be mandatory for at least one member of staff in every school.

15.   The Committee recognises the impact on curriculum development of the National Writing Project and would wish consideration to be given to a National Language Project which would encourage working groups of teachers in participating LEAs to address the issues identified in this report. A national project of this kind, under the auspices of the School Curriculum Development Committee and its successor, would stimulate much valuable classroom-based work across the country. This may well involve the setting up of an organisation separate from but working in liaison with one set up under the scheme described in the previous paragraph. Whatever the organisational framework, we believe that such a project would serve a valuable purpose. Therefore

The Committee recommends that a National Language Project be established.

16.   The single most important agency for maintaining and raising standards of achievement in schools is undoubtedly teachers themselves. One of the purposes of this report is to develop debate and discussion within the education system on the value and nature of knowledge about language. In this way it will contribute towards the professional development of teachers and an enrichment of pupils' experience. Moreover, it should be the responsibility of language consultants in primary schools, with the support of the headteachers, of heads of English departments in secondary schools, and of the academic boards (or other responsible agencies) in teacher training institutions, to ensure that the language policies of their respective institutions are expanded in the light of the report, that revised policies are implemented and that staff members are deployed to best effect. Furthermore, staff members' INSET needs for knowledge about language should be made a priority and headteachers should give it priority when deciding upon allocated INSET time in schools.

17.   Clearly, schools are dependent to a large extent on their LEAs for provision of INSET and curriculum development, and in particular on LEA advisers and inspectors working within LEA policy guidelines. It is therefore important that LEAs take an initiative to treat knowledge about language as an INSET priority. Local authorities vary considerably in size, and in the financial resources available to them; not all have advisers or inspectors with a specialist responsibility for English; some cover such a large territorial area that the organisation of INSET is particularly difficult. Nonetheless, we believe that on the staff of every authority there should be an advisory teacher, adviser or inspector, with a responsibility for developing INSET concerning knowledge about language. Those people would be expected to initiate and develop provision for teachers from each school throughout their areas.

18. We have already urged that funding for INSET in English will have to be increased. We urge that: LEAs should appreciate the importance of language study and identify it as a priority when bidding for central government funding, whether that be from funds in the Training Grants Scheme or from new sources; LEAs frame their staffing policies so as to employ suitably qualified and experienced teachers, and to enable schools to release teachers for INSET.

19. Pupils' attainments in their use and understanding of the English language can be higher than they are but only if the expectations of those who teach them are higher. In many places expectations are already high. In others, they are too low. Expectations uninformed by knowledge and understanding of how to apply that knowledge are of little value. The most important aspect of this report is the training of those who teach and are to teach. The Committee has received a great deal of evidence to show that there is much goodwill and readiness among teachers to raise teaching standards. An energetic, co-ordinated thrust is needed from providers of education at every level to inform and inspire their own profession about language knowledge. How much of that knowledge should be formally and analytically made explicit to different groups of pupils is the business of the educators themselves. But this Committee would draw attention to a key principle concerning the accessibility of knowledge about language for all. It was particularised by Margaret Donaldson in a passage addressing the relationship between written and spoken English:

It seems to be widely believed that children must not be told the truth about the system to begin with because they could not cope with such complexities. I believe this to be quite mistaken. What underlies the mistake is, I think, a failure to make a crucial distinction – a failure to see the difference between understanding the nature of the system and mastering all the individual patterns of relationship. It will inevitably take a child some time to learn all the sets of correspondences. The question is simply whether he will do this better if he is correctly informed about the kind of thing to expect.
(*Children's Minds*, Fontana/Collins, 1978, p.105)

The Committee believes that children have the right to be so informed.

Summary of recommendations

The Committee has made recommendations which address its terms of reference and has made further recommendations arising out of its work which will, in its view, help to achieve higher standards and which are capable of being implemented. The recommendations are listed below in the order in which they appear in the text. (The relevant chapter and paragraph numbers are given in brackets.)

1. The Committee recommends that the model required by the first term of reference be that presented in this report. (Chapter 3 paragraph 21)

2. The Committee recommends that all subject departments concerned with the teaching of language in secondary schools (including English – whether as a first or second language – and foreign languages, ancient or modern) develop a co-ordinated policy for language teaching. (Chapter 4 paragraph 51)

3. The Committee recommends that all primary schools should have a member of staff who is designated as a language consultant, and who has the responsibility for advising on and co-ordinating language work, including knowledge about language. (Chapter 4 paragraph 52)

4. The Committee recommends that the Secretary of State ensure that all schools should review existing provision for English to secure sufficient curriculum time to implement the findings of this report. (Chapter 4 paragraph 53)

5. The Committee recommends that the attainment targets required by the third term of reference be those set out in this report. (Chapter 5 paragraph 10)

6. The Committee recommends that the English working group should draw upon its proposed attainment targets in formulating profile components for the assessment of English in the national curriculum. (Chapter 5 paragraph 11)

7. The Committee recommends that appropriate national testing techniques be applied to language in use and that assessment of explicit knowledge about language be largely the province of individual teachers and institutions, both kinds of assessment being necessary. These principles should be reflected in the respective arrangements for coursework assessment and written examinations in the GCSE. (Chapter 5 paragraph 19)

8. The Committee recommends that all intending teachers of primary school children should undertake a language course in which the larger part of the time allocated to the course (i.e. over 50 per cent) be spent in direct tuition of knowledge about language as outlined in the model proposed in this report which is relevant to the primary school child as displayed through the attainment targets. (Chapter 6 paragraph 5)

9. The Committee recommends that all intending teachers of English in secondary schools should undertake a course which enables them to acquire, understand and make use of knowledge about language as outlined in the model proposed in this report which is relevant to the secondary school pupil as displayed through the attainment targets. (Chapter 6 paragraph 6)

10. The Committee recommends that all teacher training courses, all of which should contain a substantial component of tuition in language study, should be evaluated at regular intervals by external assessors or moderators who have both pedagogic and linguistic expertise. (Chapter 6 paragraph 7)

11. The Committee recommends that all intending secondary teachers of subjects other than English should satisfactorily complete a course on knowledge about language based on the model presented in this report relevant to their specialist subjects in pre-service training. (Chapter 6 paragraph 8)

12. The Committee recommends that all teachers in all subjects in all secondary schools should, as part of the requirements of their probationary year, be required to be engaged in some aspect of language study as it relates to their own specialist fields or subjects. (Chapter 6 paragraph 9)

13. The Committee recommends that all providers of pre-service training for the teaching profession re-design their courses for intending teachers to meet the requirements of the relevant recommendations in this report. (Chapter 6 paragraph 10)

14. The Committee recommends that before the end of the century a prerequisite for entry to the teaching profession as an English specialist should normally be a first degree in English which incorporates a study of both contemporary and historical linguistic form and use. (Chapter 6 paragraph 11)

15. The Committee recommends that English generally and knowledge about language in particular be included in the list of national priority areas under the Local Education Authority Training Grants Scheme with effect from the earliest possible date. (Chapter 6 paragraph 12)

16. The Committee recommends that the Government review the scale of provision for the Training Grants Scheme so that adequate allowance is provided for English as long as the need exists and without putting necessary in-service training in other key areas at risk. (Chapter 6 paragraph 13)

17. The Committee recommends that a nationally devised, administered and funded scheme should arrange for people with relevant expertise to provide training both for selected staff in institutions where relevant expertise does not exist, and for selected staff in schools, such training to be mandatory for at least one member of staff in every school. (Chapter 6 paragraph 14)

18. The Committee recommends that a National Language Project be established. (Chapter 6 paragraph 15)

The suggestions and recommendations we have made in this report will, if accepted and implemented, entail action at different levels. Individual teachers, schools, advisers, local authorities, teacher training institutions, universities, and central government all have parts to play. Our terms of reference did not enjoin, nor did time allow, a detailed specification and evaluation of what our recommendations imply for these different agencies. We therefore propose to the Department of Education and Science that it undertake or commission a rigorous and detailed survey of the changes we propose, with the assistance of either some members of the Committee or officials who have served the Committee, in consultation with the national curriculum working group on English.

Appendix *1*   *Terms of reference*

1. To recommend a model of the English language, whether spoken or written, which would:
   i   serve as the basis of how teachers are trained to understand how the English language works;
   ii   inform professional discussion of all aspects of English teaching.

2. To recommend the principles which should guide teachers on how far and in what ways the model should be made explicit to pupils, to make them conscious of how language is used in a range of contexts.

3. To recommend what, in general terms, pupils need to know about how the English language works and in consequence what they should have been taught, and be expected to understand, on this score, at ages 7, 11 and 16.

Membership of the Committee

Professor Gillian Brown
Professor in Applied Linguistics and Dean of the School of Social Studies, University of Essex

Mrs A. S. Byatt, FRSL
Writer, broadcaster and reviewer. Former Senior Lecturer in English, University College, London

Professor Brian Cox
John Edward Taylor Professor of English Literature and Pro-Vice-Chancellor, University of Manchester

Mr Leonard Ellis
Senior Lecturer in Education, North Riding College. Former primary school headteacher

Mr P. J. Kavanagh, FRSL
Poet, novelist and author of children's books

Sir John Kingman, FRS – **Chairman**
Vice-Chancellor, University of Bristol

Mr Richard Knott
General adviser with responsibility for English and drama, Berkshire LEA

Mrs Pramila Le Hunte
Head of English Department, The North London Collegiate School

Professor Peter Levi, FSA, FRSL
Professor of Poetry, University of Oxford, and Fellow of St Catherine's College, Oxford

Miss Patricia Mann (until August 1987)
Head of External Affairs, J Walter Thompson Group, and Editor of *Consumer Affairs*

Mr Robert Robinson
Writer and broadcaster

Mrs Jeanne Strickland
Deputy Head of Camden School for Girls, London. Former Head of English Department

Dr Charles Suckling, FRS
Former General Manager, Research and Technology, ICI PLC

Mr Keith Waterhouse, FRSL
Journalist, novelist and dramatist

Professor Henry Widdowson
Professor of Education and Head of Department of English for Speakers of Other Languages, University of London Institute of Education

Mr P. Gannon, HMI – Secretary to the Committee

Mrs R. Hussain, DES – Assistant Secretary to the Committee

Mr M. D. Phipps, DES – Assessor

Mr G. R. Frater, HIM – Observer

Because of increased professional demands on Miss Mann's time, she felt obliged to resign from the Committee in August 1987. Owing to illness, Professor Widdowson was unfortunately prevented from participating in the Committee's discussion and decisions during the last five weeks of its work.

Appendix 3 *Note of reservation*

by Professor Henry Widdowson

I am in complete agreement with my colleagues on the Committee that knowledge about language, along the lines of the model in Chapter 3 of the report, should be an essential framework of reference for the teaching of English in schools. I concur with the recommendations. But I cannot agree with the way the case has been argued: a number of crucial issues are, I believe, left unexamined and their relationship left unexplained. The intention of this note is to indicate what these issues are, not only to give reasons for my reservation but also, more positively, to extend the report by the outline of an alternative view.

The rationale for the model ought clearly to carry conviction. But as it is presented in Chapter 2, for all the interesting points it raises, it is, I think, pitched at too general and uncritical a level. This, I think, is because it does not come to grips with the central question of how knowledge about language can be shown to be relevant to the educational aims of English as a school subject.

Indeed, what these educational aims should be, what English is on the curriculum *for*, is not really explored here with any rigour, but simply asserted in very general (and traditional) terms. When this point was raised in committee, it was decided that any more radical enquiry into the purposes for English would be a distraction. I believe, on the contrary, that it was central to the Committee's concerns. For only when English has been clearly defined as a subject in relation to such purposes, when the vague notion of 'mastery' is given more specific content, can a statement be logically made about the knowledge of language that is necessary to achieve the objectives of English as a subject.

Two kinds of purpose for English are recognised in the report, but their relationship is not made explicit. One kind has to do with the functioning of language in adult life and this is dealt with summarily in seven paragraphs of introduction. The other kind, which is given primary focus, has to do with the functioning of the language in four different aspects of child development in schooling: intellectual, social, personal and aesthetic. It seems to me that a crucial question arises here, namely: how do these kinds of purpose relate? How do these different aspects of development nurtured in school actually *prepare* the pupils for the uses of language in the adult world? Adult purposes are said to determine the degree of competence in the four language skills to be aimed at by pupils. How then is the achievement of these degrees of competence in the four skills to be put into correspondence with the four aspects of development? None of these questions is addressed. None of them can be addressed, since the purposes are just not analysed in sufficient detail. Seven brief paragraphs covering the complexities of adult uses of language, for example, provide no basis whatever for the principled specification of objectives or attainment targets in respect of degrees of competence, and without such specification there is no way of deciding how far the language which is used for development in the process of schooling does prepare pupils for the language demands of adulthood.

This is a matter of considerable importance and indeed can be said to lie at the heart of the debate about the current effectiveness of English teaching in schools. It is clear from the evidence received by the Committee that people *within* education tend to think of purpose primarily in terms of the development of the child in the process of schooling whereas those *outside* education tend to think of purpose primarily in terms of adult needs which pupils have to be prepared to meet. Defining English as a subject is a matter of specifying objectives which reconcile these two general perspectives on purpose and which demonstrate how developmental work can be effective also as a projection of future needs.

A clear and well-reasoned specification of objectives along these lines would necessarily lead to the outline of a model of language relevant to their achievement. The model would emerge as an implicational function of the argument: purposes → objectives → model. But because this process is not spelled out in the report the model does not emerge as a rational conclusion: it is simply made to appear. It is said that it is 'derived from the educational aims referred to in the previous chapter' (i.e. Chapter 2) but there is no demonstration of this derivation. There is no explanation as to why the model is structured as it is. There is no systematic argument that makes explicit the connection between the four components of the model, the four linguistic skills that, at some unspecified appropriate level of competence, account for adult needs, and the four aspects of development which are to be promoted during schooling.

The *pedagogic usefulness* of the model as an auxiliary device for classroom guidance is well demonstrated in Chapter 4 of the report. For some people this will perhaps provide a cogent enough case for acceptance. But I believe that this tactical and contingent use of the model needs to be given strategic significance by reference to arguments in Chapter 2 for the essential *educational relevance* of knowledge about language in the definition of English as a subject on the curriculum. But, as I have indicated, Chapter 2 does not pursue arguments of this kind. There is no explicit set of cross-references to link these three chapters logically together. I think there should be.

Of course, given the time constraints the Committee had to work to, there are bound to be areas of enquiry left unexplored. But in my view we have left unexplored just those areas which are of particular importance in deciding on what counts as a relevant model of language for the teaching of English. This is a pity since there are reasons for supposing that such exploration would have yielded powerful support for the model that has actually been proposed. It would also have provided a set of more explicit arguments in reference to which the validity of the model could have been rationally discussed, adjustments made, alternatives suggested. It is to be hoped that the report will anyway provoke this kind of positive and critical thinking by a careful evaluation of its proposals. In a field where there is a good deal of prejudice and unfounded assertion, this could well be the most important contribution such a report could make. And in this respect I would want to subscribe to it with no reservations whatever.

Appendix 4 Sources of evidence

I Organisations, associations, institutions and other bodies which submitted written evidence

Adult Literacy and Basic Skills Unit
Ariel Trust, Liverpool
Assessment of Performance Unit
Associated Examining Board
Association for Science Education
Association of County Councils
Association of Metropolitan Authorities
Association of Metropolitan Authorities – Minority Conservative Group
Association of Polytechnic Teachers
Bedfordshire Association for the Teaching of English
Birmingham Local Education Authority
Birmingham Polytechnic, School of Linguistics and English Language
Brighton Polytechnic, Faculty of Education
British Association for Applied Linguistics
British Broadcasting Corporation
British Council
Cambridge Seminar
Centre for Urban Educational Studies
Chester Association for the Teaching of English
Clwyd Branch of the National Association for the Teaching of English
College of Preceptors
Committee for Linguistics in Education
Confederation of British Industry
Council for National Academic Awards
County Educational Research and Development Centre, St Albans College, Hertfordshire
Coventry English Teachers
Cumbria Local Education Authority
Department of Education for Northern Ireland
Development of University English Teaching Project
Educational Publishers Council, English Panel
Engineering Professors' Conference
English Association
Girls' Schools Association
Hawbush Primary School, Headteacher and Staff
Headmasters' Conference
Historical Association
House of Lords (debate on the English Language)
Incorporated Association of Preparatory Schools
Independent Broadcasting Authority
Independent Schools Association Incorporated
Inner London Education Authority Secondary English Inspectors and Advisory Team
Institute of Scientific and Technical Communicators
Institution of Agricultural Engineers
Joint Association of Classical Teachers
Joint Council of Language Associations
JMB Staged Assessment in Literacy Project, Department of Education, University of Manchester

Leicestershire Branch of the National Association for the Teaching of
    English
Library Association
Linguistics Association of Great Britain
London Borough of Barnet, Education Department
London Borough of Croydon, Education Department
London Borough of Havering, Heads of English
London Borough of Merton, Teachers of English
London Borough of Newham, Education Department
Merseyside Chamber of Commerce and Industry
Midlands English Advisers
National Anti-Racist Movement in Education
National Association for Primary Education
National Association for the Teaching of English
National Association of Advisers for Computers in Education
National Association of Advisers in English
National Association of Head Teachers
National Association of Inspectors and Advisers
National Association of Language in Education Centres
National Association of Schoolmasters and Union of Women Teachers
National Confederation of Parent-Teacher Associations
National Congress on Languages in Education
National Council of Teachers of English (USA)
National Union of Teachers
National Writing Project in Dorset
Newcastle upon Tyne Polytechnic, Department of Education Studies,
    Language and Literature staff team
Norfolk and Norwich English Association
North Eastern Association for the Teaching of English
North London Collegiate School, Assistant English Teachers
Open University
Professional Association of Teachers
Queen's English Society
Reading and District Branch of the National Association for the Teaching
    of English
Rotherham Curriculum Review Group and Rotherham Heads of English
Royal Air Force
Royal Army Educational Corps
Royal Navy
Royal Society of Arts Examinations Board
Rugby Group Heads of English
School Curriculum Development Committee
School Curriculum Development Committee, National Writing Project
Schools' Poetry Association
Schools Prolog Information Retrieval and Learning Project Team,
    University of Leicester, School of Education
Scottish Education Department, HMI (Scotland)
Scottish Examination Board
Secondary Examinations Council
Secondary Heads Association
Shakespeare and Schools Project
Sheena Simon College, English Department
Sheffield City Polytechnic, Department of English
Shropshire Branch of the National Association for the Teaching of English
Simplified Spelling Society
Society of Education Officers
Society of Headmasters of Independent Schools

Somerset Heads of English
Standing Conference of Heads of English in Public Sector Higher
    Education
Standing Conference on University Entrance
Thames Television Education Department
United Kingdom i.t.a. Federation
United Kingdom Reading Association
University of Durham, School of Education
University of Lancaster, Department of Linguistics and Modern English
    Language
University of Leicester, School of Education, PGCE Primary Tutors
University of London Institute of Education, English Department MA
    Students
University of London Institute of Education, Joint Department of English
    and Media Studies
University of London School Examinations Board
University of Southampton, Centre for Language in Education (In-Service
    Course Participants)
Verbal Arts Association
Walsall Branch of the National Association for the Teaching of English
Walsall Heads of English
Welsh Office, HMI (Wales)
Wigan Language Project
Wiltshire Oracy Project
Wolverhampton Branch of the National Association for the Teaching of
    English

Local education authorities which responded to the Committee's request for details of in-service training provision for language

Cleveland
Cornwall
Cumbria
East Sussex
Inner London Education Authority
Leicestershire
Manchester
Newham
Norfolk
Richmond
Sheffield
Staffordshire
Wiltshire

A large number of providers of teacher training took the trouble to respond to the Committee's request for information about the language element of teacher training courses. The Committee is most grateful to them.

II Individuals who submitted written evidence

Posts attributed to witnesses are, unless otherwise stated, those believed to have been held at the time evidence was submitted. Where names are grouped, they were joint signatories.

Mr Peter Abbs, Lecturer in Education, University of Sussex
Mrs Joan Baker, Ms Shirley Davis and Ms Barbara Hubberstey, teachers,
    Chestreham School, Chesham, Bucks
Mr John Bald, Tutor-in-charge, Reading and Language Centre, Colchester
    Institute
Mr Lawrence Bampton, Headmaster and, formerly, member of JMB
    English Subjects and Advanced Level Committees

Mr Douglas Barnes, Reader, School of Education, University of Leeds

Dr Roger Beard, Lecturer in Primary Education, School of Education, University of Leeds

Mr Alan Beattie, Senior Lecturer in Education and Head of Health and Welfare Studies, University of London Institute of Education

Mr Mervyn Benford, Assistant Primary Adviser, Oxfordshire

Mrs June Benn, writer, formerly teacher

Mr Bob Bibby, English Adviser, Dudley

Dr Thomas Bloor, Lecturer in Linguistics, Modern Languages Department, University of Aston

Mr Waltraud Boxall, Ms Jane Pearce, Ms Eleanor Wright, Lecturers, Department of Education, University of Liverpool

Mr Dennis Brook, County English Adviser for Derbyshire

Professor E. H. Brown, Professor of Structural Analysis, Imperial College of Science and Technology, on behalf of a group of senior engineering professors

Professor Christopher Brumfit, Head of the Department of Education, University of Southampton

Mr E. James Burton, author and formerly Registrar of the Society of Teachers of Speech and Drama

Mr Neil Carpenter, teacher and researcher

Ms Elizabeth Carrier, Language Co-ordinator, Highgate Primary School, Dudley

Dr Ronald Carter, Lecturer, Department of English Studies, University of Nottingham

Mrs S. M. Castle, Middle School Teacher with responsibility for language development

Mrs Jennifer V. Chew, English teacher, Strode's Sixth Form College

Dr Edward Chitham, teacher trainer, formerly teacher

Dr Jennifer Coates, Ms Deborah Cameron and Dr Ruth Riley, Lecturers in English Language and Linguistics, Roehampton Institute

Professor N. E. Collinge, Mont Follick Professor of Comparative Philology, Department of General Linguistics, University of Manchester

Ms Margaret Cook, General Adviser with special responsibility for language development, Sefton

Mr Christopher H. Copeman, English Teacher, The Beacon School, Amersham

Dr Tony Crowley, Lecturer, Department of English, University of Southampton

Professor David Crystal, Honorary Professor of Linguistics, University College of North Wales

Mr H. Cunnington, formerly Head of English, South East Essex Sixth Form College

Ms Hilary Curwell, EFL Teacher and Adult Literacy Tutor, London

Mr Peter Dale, writer, editor, Poet-in-school and Head of English

Mrs Patricia M. Davidson, Head of English in a middle school, Hertfordshire

Mr T. T. L. Davidson, Lecturer, Department of Linguistics and Phonetics, University of Leeds

Mr Joseph Davies, primary school teacher, Coventry

Ms Annabelle Dixon, Deputy Head, Holbrook JMI School and Ms Elizabeth Hope, teacher, Puller Memorial JMI School, Hertfordshire

Miss Gillian Donmall, Director, Language Awareness Centre, King's College London

Mrs Susan Doughty, Checkpoint Computers Ltd

Mrs Ann Dummett, formerly Director of the Runnymede Trust, formerly research worker for the Joint Council for the Welfare of Immigrants, and member of the Swann Committee of Inquiry into the Education of Ethnic Minority Groups' Children

Ms Hazel Elliot-Kemp, Helios Education and Management Consultants

Ms Irene Farrell, Open University student, London

Professor P. B. Fellgett, Head of the Department of Cybernetics, University of Reading

Ms Irene Finch, Home Economics teacher, London

Professor Boris Ford, Emeritus Professor of Education, University of Bristol

Mr Harold Gardiner, formerly HMI Staff Inspector for English

Dr T. P. Gorman, Head of the Department of Language, and Ms J. White, Senior Research Officer, National Foundation for Educational Research

Mr T. Greaves, retired teacher

Professor Sidney Greenbaum, Quain Professor of English Language and Literature, University College, London

Mr P. H. Griffith, Director of Professional Development in Education, Open University

Dr Dennis Hamley, County English Adviser, and Dr Richard Anderson, Adviser for English, Hertfordshire

Dr John Harris, Lecturer, Department of Phonetics and Linguistics, University College, London

Professor Eric Hawkins, Emeritus Professor, University of York, and Honorary Professor, University College of Wales, Aberystwyth

Professor Philip Hobsbaum, Titular Professor, Department of English Literature, University of Glasgow

Mr A. Wyn Hobson, Head of English, Ysgol Dyffryn Ogwen, Bethesda, Gywnedd

Professor R. M. Hogg, Smith Professor of English Language and Medieval Literature, University of Manchester

Mr R. L. Houghton, English teacher, William Hulme's Independent School

Mrs M. M. Hubner, English teacher, Bishop Stopford School, Kettering

Dr Richard Hudson, Reader in Linguistics, Department of Phonetics and Linguistics, University College, London, and Editor of CLIE papers

Mr Adrian Ingham, Headteacher, Cranford Park Junior School, Hillingdon

Dr A. G. James, Principal Lecturer, Edge Hill College of Higher Education

Dr P. V. Jones, Senior Lecturer in Classics, University of Newcastle upon Tyne, and Mr A. J. Spooner, Head of Classics, Park View Comprehensive School, Co. Durham

Mr George R. Keith, Director, Cheshire Language Centre, North Cheshire College

Mr J. Kelly, Senior Lecturer, and Dr A. R. Warner, Lecturer, Board of Studies in Language and Linguistic Science, University of York

Dr P. E. Kerswill, Lecturer in Linguistic Science, University of Reading

Mr D. Kirkham, Head of English, Newport Free Grammar School, Essex

Mr Roger Knight, Senior Lecturer in Education, University of Leicester, and Editor of *The Use of English*

Dr B. C. Lamb, Lecturer in Life Sciences, Imperial College of Science and Technology

Miss Marghanita Laski, novelist, critic and journalist (deceased)

Mrs S. J. Lloyd, teacher, Woods Loke Primary School, Suffolk

Mrs Mona McNee, Norfolk

Mr G. Maddicks, Bristol

Mr K. P. Maloney, Headmaster, Tenter Fields Primary School, Dudley

Ms Clare Mar-Molinero, Lecturer in Spanish, University of Southampton

Dr John Marenbon, Centre for Policy Studies, Fellow and Director of Studies in English, Trinity College, Cambridge

Miss Nancy Martin and Professor James Britton, formerly associated with the teaching of English at the University of London Institute of Education, and Mrs Pat D'Arcy, English Adviser, Wiltshire LEA

Dr Lesley Milroy, Senior Lecturer, Department of Speech, University of Newcastle upon Tyne

Dr W. H. Mittins, formerly Head of Division (Higher Degrees and Research) School of Education, University of Newcastle upon Tyne

Dr Joyce M. Morris, author and Language Arts Consultant

Mr D. V. Moseley, Reader in Applied Psychology, University of Newcastle upon Tyne

Dame Iris Murdoch, novelist and philosopher

Professor N. E. Osselton, Professor of English Language, University of Newcastle upon Tyne

Dr D. E. Packham, Senior Lecturer in Materials Science, University of Bath

Mr John Pearce, Senior Inspector, Cambridgeshire LEA

Mrs Katharine Perera, Lecturer, Department of Linguistics, University of Manchester

Mr A. E. Phipps, Head of English, Smethwick Hall Boys' High School, Sandwell

Ms Pamela Pink, Head of English, Rooks Heath High School, Harrow

Mr M. D. Preston, postgraduate student, Garnett College

Mr Nigel Proctor, Department of Arts and Humanities Education, Manchester Polytechnic

Dr Robert Protherough, Senior Lecturer responsible for English, School of Education, University of Hull

Sir Randolph Quirk, author, President of the British Academy, and Fellow of University College, London

Ms Pauline C. Robinson, Lecturer, Centre for Applied Language Studies, University of Reading

Mr Omer Roucoux, Science teacher, Manshead Upper School, Bedfordshire

Mr Edward Rowney, retired English teacher, Louth, Lincolnshire

Professor G. R. Sampson, Professor of Linguistics and Head of the Department of Linguistics and Phonetics, University of Leeds

Mr P. J. Scholfield, Lecturer, Department of Linguistics, University College of North Wales

Mr David Self, freelance writer, formerly English teacher and Lecturer

Mrs C. M. Sewell, Head of English, Tudhoe Grange Comprehensive School, Co. Durham

Professor Robert E. Shafer, Professor of English Education, Department of English, Arizona State University, USA

Mr E. D. Shaw, Chairman of the Society of Teachers of Speech and Drama

Mr N. F. Sherman, teacher, St Richard's Primary School, Dover

Professor J. McH. Sinclair, Professor of Modern English Language, Department of English Language and Literature, University of Birmingham

Mr Leslie Stratta, formerly Senior Lecturer in English in Education, University of Birmingham, and Mr John Dixon, formerly Director of the Diploma in English Studies, University of Leeds

Mr Richard Stroud, Hereford

Mr C. W. Taylor, formerly polytechnic Lecturer

Mrs Jocelyn Underwood, teacher of special needs pupils

Mr Peter R. Walker, Head of English, Hounslow Manor School

Mr Colin Walter, teacher, School of Education, Goldsmiths' College, University of London

Mr G. G. Watkins, Senior English Master and Senior Teacher (Arts), The Royal Grammar School, Lancaster

Miss B. Weatherall, Head of English, Portslade Community College, East Sussex

Mr John Welch, Director, National Association for Gifted Children

Mrs Lyn Wendon, Letterland Ltd, Cambridge

Professor Andrew M. Wilkinson, Professor of Education, University of East Anglia

Ms Valerie Yule, Honorary Research Fellow, Department of Psychology, University of Aberdeen

In addition, the Committee received 205 letters offering helpful comments and advice.

III Written evidence from H M Inspectorate	HMI – English Committee HMI – Education and Ethnic Diversity Committee HMI – Primary Committee HMI – Teacher Training Committee
Written evidence from individual members of H M Inspectorate	Mr G. R. Frater, HMI Mr J. Fitzpatrick, HMI Mr S. J. A. Rogers, HMI
IV Organisations which gave oral evidence	National Association for the Teaching of English represented by: Ms M. Barrs Mr T. Furlong Mr K. Kimberley

National Anti-racist Movement in Education represented by:
Mr R. Blackman
Ms R. Garside
Mr S. Shukla

National Association of Advisers in English represented by:
Mr D. Allen
Mr B. Moorhouse
Mrs J. Thexton

National Association of Head Teachers represented by:
Mr A. De Caux
Mrs S. Pollock
Miss M. Sedgwick
Mr D. Tracey

National Congress for Languages in Education represented by:
Miss G. Donmall
Mr R. Hardie
Professor J. McH. Sinclair

Task Group on Assessment and Testing represented by:
Professor P. Black (Chairman)
Dr C. Burstall
Mr T. Christie
Mrs D. Kavanagh
Mrs H. Steedman

United Kingdom Reading Association represented by:
Mr D. Dennis
Dr C. Harrison
Mrs M. Hunter-Carsch

V Individuals who gave oral evidence	Mr E. J. Bolton, CB, Senior Chief Inspector – H M Inspectorate Mrs K. Perera, Lecturer, Department of Linguistics, University of Manchester
VI Individuals who have provided helpful advice and support	Mr R. Arnold, formerly HMI and now English Adviser for Oxfordshire Professor R. Blin-Stoyle, FRS, Professor of Theoretical Physics, University of Sussex, and Chairman of the School Curriculum Development Committee Mr N. Brown, Lecturer in Russian, University of London, School of Slavonic and Eastern European Studies Miss S. J. Browne, CB, formerly Senior Chief Inspector – H M Inspectorate and now Principal of Newnham College, Cambridge Sir W. Cockcroft, Chairman and Chief Executive of the Secondary Examinations Council Dr H. Dombey, Chairperson of the National Association for the Teaching of English Mr D. Halligan, HMI Mr D. Mathews, Lecturer in Urdu, University of London, School of Oriental and African Studies Professor M. Stubbs, Department of English and Media Studies, University of London Institute of Education Mrs S. P. Twite, HMI

Their contributions to the work of the Committee have been invaluable.

Members of the **Department of Education and Science** helped in various ways, and we are particularly grateful for the co-operation of staff in the Department's Library, and in its Printing and Committee sections.

Appendix 5   *Visits by members of the Committee*

I   Secondary school visits

Local education authority	School	Head
Birmingham	Holte School	Mr G. C. Gray
Cambridgeshire	Comberton Village College	Mrs R. Clayton
	King's Church of England School	Mr M. J. Barcroft
Coventry	Whitley Abbey Comprehensive School	Mr O. Shelton
Cumbria	John Ruskin School	Mr R. J. Jarratt
	Queen Katherine School	Mrs M. M. Davies
Devon	Exmouth Community College	Mr P. E. Thorne
Durham	Sedgefield Community College	Mr A. F. Williams
ILEA	Archbishop Michael Ramsey School	Mrs S. Hace
	Mulberry School for Girls	Mrs D. J. E. Gould
	North Westminster Community School	Mr M. Marland, CBE
Lincolnshire	Caistor Grammar School	Mr T. J. Foulkes
Northumberland	King Edward VI School	Mr M. N. Duffy
Wirral	Prenton Girls' High School	Miss S. Goodall
Independent schools	The Maynard School for Girls, Devon	Miss F. Murdin
	The Oratory School for Boys, Reading	Mr A. J. Snow

II   Primary school visits

Local education authority	School	Head
Birmingham	St Saviour's Church of England Primary School	Mrs C. E. Evans
Essex	Mountnessing Church of England Primary School	Mrs C. J. Rosslyn
Kent	St Mildred's Infant School	Mrs B. J. Regan (acting)
Liverpool	Tiber Street Junior School	Miss J. Price
Newham	Ravenscroft Infant School	Mrs M. B. Hadson
North Yorkshire	Ainderby Steeple Church of England Primary School	Mrs P. Graham
	Dringhouses Primary School	Mr J. Copley
Oxfordshire	Wheatley Primary School	Mr C. Hallett
Salford	St Luke's with All Saints Church of England Primary School	Mr L. Duffy
Shropshire	St George's Junior School	Mrs A. Oliver
Suffolk	Halesworth Middle School	Mr B. E. Bugg
West Sussex	Laburnham Grove Junior School	Mr A. S. Fitzgerald
Wiltshire	Frogwell Primary School	Mr E. M. Shaw (since retired)
	Northview Primary School	Mrs J. Jarvis

III Teacher training establishments visited

University Departments of Education

Department of Education University of Cambridge	Head of Department Professor P. Hirst
School of Education University of Nottingham	Chairman of School Professor P. Gammage

Polytechnic Departments of Education

Faculty of Education Brighton Polytechnic	Dean of Faculty Mr K. L. Gardner
Department of English Sheffield City Polytechnic	Head of Department Mrs M. Ainsworth

Colleges of Higher Education Departments of Education

School of Education Essex Institute of Higher Education	Head of School Dr N. Ferguson
School of Education and Teaching Studies Worcester College of Higher Education	Dean of School Rev. Dr D. Sharples

Appendix 6 Glossary of terms used in Chapter 3

Some terms used in the model (Figures 1–5) may not be familiar to readers. This glossary provides brief definitions. Terms which may be assumed to be known (however specifically defined) such as *verb, noun, adjective, metaphor, negation*, etc. are not included. In any case, all terms used in Chapter 3 are either explained in the text of the report, can be found by reference to the works cited in the bibliography (Appendix 7), or are listed below.

Adjunct: a kind of adverbial (q.v.) which is a major constituent of a sentence or clause, e.g. 'he was writing *indoors*'.

Adverbial: a general term for that constituent of a sentence which is distinct from subject, object, verb, and complement. There are three kinds of adverbials, viz. adjuncts (q.v.), conjuncts (q.v.) and disjuncts (q.v.).

Anaphora: the process of referring to what has already been mentioned. In the sentence 'I had another key but I've lost it' the word *it* refers anaphorically to *another key*. Any item referred to may occur earlier in the same utterance or in a previous utterance. The understanding of anaphoric reference is obviously of importance in the accurate use of pronouns.

Antonymy: the relationship between words or expressions which contrast in meaning. The most obvious kind of antonymy is where the contrast is one of opposition. A person is either alive or dead: *dead* is an antonym in respect of *alive*. But there are other kinds of antonyms (a more general term than 'opposites') as in converse terms such as *buy* and *sell*, or so-called *gradable antonyms*, like *good* and *bad*, where gradations of goodness or badness may be being contrasted. *Antonymy* is a general term covering all of these.

Apposition: the use of different linguistic forms of distinct semantic content (be they words, phrases or clauses) which have the same syntactic form or function. Thus in the sentence 'I have just met the new head of department, a remarkable woman' the terms *head of department* and *a remarkable woman* are in apposition, since they have the same grammatical function (object of the verb) but not the same semantic content even though both refer to the same person.

Cohesion: a general term for the grammatical and semantic relations by which one part of a discourse (q.v.) is linked to other parts which precede or succeed it. In the following – 'Last night I met a very interesting chap. He was telling me about his job as a lumberjack' there is cohesion between the two sentences through the relationship between *chap, he*, and *his*.

Collocation: the way in which some words regularly keep company with other words in contexts of use. So there is a relationship of collocation between *fork, spoon, dish, napkin, tablecloth*, etc.

Conjunct: a kind of adverbial (q.v.) which is outside the main structure of a sentence or clause, and which connects what is being said to what was said before, as in 'If you ask her for a loan, *then* I'm sure she'll give it to you'.

Co-ordination: the linking of two forms of language (whether they be words, phrases or sentences) in such a way as to make them independent elements of a single constituent. The most obvious example is by means of *and*, as in 'Peter *and* Paul left school together', where *Peter* and *Paul* together form the constituent which is also the subject of the sentence. Co-ordination can occur at all levels of analysis.

Deixis (adj. deictic): deictic expressions are words and phrases whose interpretation requires a knowledge of who the speaker/writer is, and the time and place of utterance (e.g. *I, we, our, here, now, to my left*) .

Demonstrative: a word which can function either as part of a noun phrase, as in '*This* book is the best I've read this year' or as a pronoun, as in '*That* is the best book I've read this year'. As the term 'demonstrative' suggests, it usually points to or indicates some specific item (see *deixis*).

Discourse: a connected stretch of language in use. The term applies to both spoken and written language, and thus a piece of discourse may be of any length. Paragraphs, public notices, chapters, whole books, conversations, formal lectures, a friendly exchange of greetings are all examples of discourse.

Disjunct: a kind of adverbial (q.v.) which is not part of a sentence or clause. There is usually some evaluative content in the meaning of disjuncts e.g. '*Unfortunately*, he wasn't at home'. Disjuncts can consist of phrases as well as words, as in '*To be honest with you*, I think you look very ill'.

Ellipsis: The omission of a word or words which would be necessary for complete grammaticality in a sentence, but is not needed for expressing an intended meaning in context.

Given and **new**: these everyday words have a technical meaning when describing language in use. Information presented by a speaker (or writer) can be separated into what the speaker wishes you to 'attend to' – the *new* – and the *given* constitutes what is known or knowable by the listener (or reader) at a particular point in the discourse. So in 'The proposal you put forward has been accepted' – *The proposal you put forward* is *given*, and *has been accepted* is *new*. There is a close but not isomorphic relation between *given/new* and the traditional semantic categories of *subject/predicate*.

Hyponymy: the relation between a specific term and a general term which includes the meaning of the specific term. The specific term is referred to as a hyponym, so that a *St Bernard* is a hyponym of *dog*, just as *dog* is, in turn, a hyponym of *animal*.

Inflection: the addition of endings to a word in order to express grammatical categories like tense and number: for example, *s* is the inflection in the word *arrives*, which makes it a third person singular form. English is a relatively uninflected language compared with many others.

Lexis: the area of language study concerned with words and their meanings. A lexical study of language is one which is concerned with vocabulary rather than with grammar.

Modal: an auxiliary verb indicating judgement and attitude, i.e. whether the proposition expressed is to be considered a fact, or a wish, or a possibility. There is a very small number of modal auxiliaries in English (*can, could, may, might, should, must*, etc.).

Referent: that which is being referred to. Semantically – the object or concept denoted by a word or expression to which reference is made.

Referring expression: a word or phrase which refers to individuals, objects or events which have already been referred to in the discourse, or are believed to be known by the reader/listener. Thus, in 'The cat's got out again: we'll have to have it neutered' *the cat, we* and *it* are all referring expressions.

Subordination: the linking of two forms of language (whether they be words, phrases or sentences) in such a way that one item is dependent for its function on (or subordinate to) the other. So, in the sentence '*Although the school was four miles away* they walked each way' the italicised clause is subordinated to the main clause. Subordination contrasts with co-ordination (q.v.) – cf. *The school was four miles away* but *they walked each way* where each clause remains independent of the other.

Appendix 7 *Bibliography to supplement Chapter 3*

We begin by proposing some books with very wide coverage as an orientation to the study of language. (In all cases, date of publication refers to the most recent edition.)

Bolinger, D. L. and Sears, D. A. (1981) *Aspects of language* Harcourt Brace Jovanovich

Hawkins, E. (1987) *Awareness of language: An introduction* Cambridge University Press

Quirk, R. (1968) *Use of English* Longman

Yule, G. (1985) *Study of language: An introduction* Cambridge University Press

Figure 1: Forms of language

Figure 1 Box 1

Brazil, D., Coulthard, M. and Johns, C. (1980) *Discourse, intonation and language teaching* Longman

Brown, G. (1977) *Listening to spoken English* Longman

Crystal, D. (1975) *English tone of voice: Essays in intonation, prosody and paralanguage* Edward Arnold

Fudge, E. C. (1984) *English word stress* Allen and Unwin

Gimson, A. C. (1980) *Introduction to the pronunciation of English* Edward Arnold

O'Connor, J. D. (1973) *Phonetics* Penguin

Quirk, R. and Greenbaum, S. (1973) *University grammar of English* Longman

Turner, G. W. (1973) *Stylistics* Penguin, ch. 2

Wells, J. C. (1982) *Accents of English* Cambridge University Press (3 vols.)

Figure 1 Box 2

Albrow, K. H. (1972) *The English writing system: Notes towards a description* Schools Council: Longman

Baugh, A. C. and Cable, T. (1978) *History of the English language* Routledge and Kegan Paul

Diringer, D. (1962) *Writing* Thames and Hudson

Frith, U. (ed.) (1980) *Cognitive processes in spelling* Academic Press

Gelb, I. J. (1952) *Study of writing* University of Chicago Press

Halliday, M. A. K. (1985) *Spoken and written language* Deakin University Press

Jarman, C. (1979) *The development of handwriting skills* Blackwell

Perera, K. (1984) *Children's writing and reading: Analysing classroom language* Blackwell

Sampson, G. (1985) *Writing systems* Hutchinson

Scragg, D. G. (1975) *History of English spelling* Manchester University Press

Stubbs, M. (1980) *Language and literacy: The sociolinguistics of reading and writing* Routledge and Kegan Paul

Venezky, R. L. (1970) *The structure of English orthography* Mouton

Figure 1 Box 3

Adams, V. (1976) *Introduction to modern English word formation* Longman

Aitchison, J. (1987) *Words in the mind: An introduction to the mental lexicon* Blackwell

Allan, K. (1986) *Linguistic meaning* Routledge and Kegan Paul (2 vols.)

Bauer, L. (1983) *English word-formation* Cambridge University Press

Carter, R. and McCarthy, M. (1988) *Vocabulary and language learning* Longman

Cruse, D. A. (1986) *Lexical semantics* Cambridge University Press

Gairns, R. and Redman, S. (1986) *Working with words: Guide to teaching and learning vocabulary* Cambridge University Press

Hurford, J. R. and Heasley, B. (1983) *Semantics: A coursebook* Cambridge University Press

Ilson, R. (ed.) (1985) *Dictionaries, lexicography and language learning* Pergamon Press

Lakoff, G. and Johnson, M. (1980) *Metaphors we live by* University of Chicago Press

Leach, G. (1974) *Semantics* Penguin

Lyons, J. (1977) *Semantics* Cambridge University Press, vols.1 and 2

Matthews, P. H. (1974) *Morphology: Introduction to the theory of word structure* Cambridge University Press

Ortony, A. (ed.) (1979) *Metaphor and thought* Cambridge University Press

Palmer, F. R. (1981) *Semantics: A new outline* Cambridge University Press

Quirk, R. and Greenbaum, S. (1973) *University grammar of English* Longman

Figure 1 Box 4
Allerton, D. J. (1979) *Essentials of grammatical theory: A consensus view of syntax and morphology* Routledge and Kegan Paul

Crystal, D. (1988) *The English language* Penguin

Gannon, P. and Czerniewska, P. (1980) *Using linguistics: An educational focus* Edward Arnold

Leech, G. (1982) *English grammar for today: New introduction* Macmillan

Leech, G. N. (1972) *Meaning and the English verb* Longman

Leech, G. N. and Svartvik, J. (1975) *Communicative grammar of English* Longman

Palmer, F. (1988 forthcoming) *The English verb* Longman

Perera, K. (1984) *Children's writing and reading: Analysing classroom language* Blackwell, ch. 2

Quirk, R. and Greenbaum, S. (1973) *University grammar of English* Longman

Winter, E. (1982) *Towards a contextual grammar of English* Allen and Unwin

Young, D. J. (1984) *Introducing English grammar* Hutchinson Education

Figure 1 Box 5
Allan, K. (1986) *Linguistic meaning* Routledge and Kegan Paul (2 vols.)

Brown, G. and Yule, G. (1983) *Discourse analysis* Cambridge University Press

De Beaugrande, R. A. and Dressler, W. U. (1981) *Introduction to text linguistics* Longman

Goffman, E. (1981) *Forms of talk* Blackwell

Gumperz, J. J. (1982) *Discourse strategies* Cambridge University Press

Halliday, M. A. K. and Hasan, R. (1976) *Cohesion in English* Longman

Hoey, M. (1983) *On the surface of discourse* Allen and Unwin

Levinson, S. C. (1983) *Pragmatics* Cambridge University Press

Quirk, R. (1987) *Words at work: Lectures on textual structure* Longman

Quirk, R. and Greenbaum, S. (1973) *University grammar of English* Longman

Stubbs, M. (1983) *Discourse analysis: The sociolinguistic analysis of natural language* Blackwell

van Dijk, Teun A. (1980) *Text and context: Explorations in the semantics and pragmatics of discourse* Longman

Widdowson, H. G. (1983) *Learning purpose and language use* Oxford University Press

Figures 2 and 3: Communication and comprehension
Figure 2: Communication

Brown, P. and Levinson, S. C. (1987) *Politeness* Cambridge University Press

Bygate, M. (1987) *Speaking* Oxford University Press

Grice, P. (1975) 'Logic and conversation' in P. Cole and J. L. Morgan (eds.) *Syntax and semantics* vol.3: *Speech acts* Academic Press

Gumperz, J. J. (1982) *Discourse strategies* Cambridge University Press

Hudson, R. A. (1980) *Sociolinguistics* Cambridge University Press

Kress, G. (1982) *Learning to write* Routledge and Kegan Paul

Lyons, J. (1981) *Language, meaning and context* Fontana

Milroy, J. and Milroy, L. (1985) *Authority in language: Investigating language standardisation and prescription* Routledge and Kegan Paul

Montgomery, M. (1985) *Introduction to language and society* Methuen

O'Donnell, W. R. and Todd, L. (1980) *Variety in contemporary English* Allen and Unwin

Ong, W. J. (1982) *Orality and literacy* Methuen

Richards, J. C. and Schmidt, R. W. (eds.) (1983) *Language and communication* Longman

Saville-Troike, M. (1982) *Ethnography of communication* Blackwell

Shaughnessy, M. (1977) *Errors and expectations* Oxford University Press

Sinclair, J. McH. and Brazil, D. (1982) *Teacher talk* Oxford University Press

Smith, F. (1982) *Writing and the writer* Heinemann

Wardhaugh, R. (1985) *How conversation works* Blackwell

Widdowson, H. G. (1978) *Teaching language as communication* Oxford University Press

Figure 3: Comprehension

Aitchison, J. (1976) *Articulate mammal: Introduction to psycholinguistics* Hutchinson Education

Allan, K. (1986) *Linguistic meaning* Routledge and Kegan Paul (2 vols.)

Anderson, A. and Lynch, A. (1988 forthcoming) *Listening* Oxford University Press

Brown, G. and Yule, G. (1983) *Discourse analysis* Cambridge University Press

Carter, R. (ed.) (1982) *Language and literature: An introductory reader in stylistics* Allen and Unwin

Clark, H. H. and Clark, E. V. (1977) *Psychology and language: Introduction to psycholinguistics* Harcourt Brace Jovanovich

Cluysenaar, A. A. A. (1976) *Introduction to literary stylistics* Batsford

Edwards, D. and Mercer, N. (1987) *Common knowledge: The development of understanding in the classroom* Methuen

Garnham, A. (1985) *Psycholinguistics* Methuen

Harrison, C. (1980) *Readability in the classroom* Cambridge University Press

Leech, G. N. and Short, M. H. (1981) *Style in fiction: A linguistic introduction to English fictional prose* Longman

Levinson, S. C. (1983) *Pragmatics* Cambridge University Press

Lunzer, E. and Gardner, K. *The effective use of reading* Heinemann Educational

Sanford, A. J. and Garrod, S. C. (1981) *Understanding written language: Exploration of comprehension beyond the sentence* John Wiley

Sperber, D. and Wilson, D. (1986) *Relevance: Communication and cognition* Blackwell

Strickland, G. (1981) *Structuralism or criticism?: Thoughts on how we read* Cambridge University Press

Stubbs, M. (1983) *Discourse analysis: The sociolinguistic analysis of natural language* Blackwell

Widdowson, H. G. (1975) *Stylistics and the teaching of literature* Longman

Figure 4: Language acquisition and development

Aitchison, J. (1976) *Articulate mammal: Introduction to psycholinguistics* Hutchinson Education

Brice-Heath, S. (1983) *Ways with words: Language, life and work in communities and classrooms* Cambridge University Press

Brown, R. (1974) *First language: Early stages* Allen and Unwin

Bruner, J. S. (1975) 'Language as an instrument of thought' in Davies, A. (ed.) *Problems of language and learning* Heinemann Educational

Clark, H. H. and Clark, E. V. (1977) *Psychology and language: Introduction to psycholinguistics* Harcourt Brace Jovanovich

Dale, P. S. (1976) *Language development: Structure and function* Holt, Rinehart and Winston

Davies, A. (ed.) (1977) *Language and learning in early childhood* Heinemann Educational

Donaldson, M. (1984) *Children's minds* Fontana

Donaldson, Morag (1986) *Children's explanations: A psycholinguistic study* Cambridge University Press

Durkin, K. (1986) *Language development in the school years* Croom Helm

Edwards, J. R. (1979) *Language and disadvantage* Edward Arnold

Fletcher, P. J. and Garman, M. (eds.) (1979) *Language acquisition: Studies in first language development* Cambridge University Press

Gordon, J. (1981) *Verbal defect: A critique* Croom Helm

Halliday, M. A. K. (1975) *Learning how to mean* Edward Arnold

Luria, A. R. and Yudovich, F. Ia. (1978) *Speech and the development of mental processes in the child* Penguin

Olson, D. R., Torrance, N. and Hildyard, A. (1985) *Literacy, language and learning: The nature and consequences of reading and writing* Cambridge University Press

Perera, K. (1984) *Children's writing and reading: Analysing classroom language* Blackwell

Rogers, S. (ed.) (1976) *They don't speak our language: Essays on the language world of children and adolescents* Edward Arnold

Romaine, S. (1984) *Language of children and adolescents: The acquisition of communicative competence* Blackwell

Tizard, B. and Hughes, M. (1984) *Young children learning: Talking and thinking at home and at school* Fontana

Vygotsky, L. S. (1962) *Thought and language* Massachusetts Institute of Technology Press

Wells, G. (1985) *Language Development in the pre-school years* Cambridge University Press

Wells, G. (1987) *The meaning makers* Hodder and Stoughton

Figure 5: Geographical and historical variation
Geographical variation

Bell, R. T. (1976) *Sociolinguistics: Goals, approaches and problems* Batsford

Dittmar, N. (1976) *Sociolinguistics: A critical survey of theory and application* Edward Arnold

Edwards, V. (1979) *The West Indian language issue in British schools: Challenges and responses* Routledge and Kegan Paul

Hudson, R. A. (1980) *Sociolinguistics* Cambridge University Press

Hughes, A. and Trudgill, P. (1979) *English accents and dialects* Edward Arnold

Kachru, B. B. (1986) *Alchemy of English* Pergamon Press

Linguistic Minorities Project (1983) *Linguistic minorities in England* Heinemann Educational

Linguistic Minorities Project (1985) *Other languages of England* Routledge and Kegan Paul

Montgomery, M. (1985) *Introduction to language and society* Methuen

Quirk, R. and Widdowson, H. G. (eds.) (1985) *English in the world: Teaching and learning the language and literature* Cambridge University Press

Rosen, H. and Burgess, T. (1980) *Languages and dialects in London schoolchildren: An investigation* Ward Lock Educational

Suttcliffe, D. (1983) *British Black English* Blackwell

Suttcliffe, D. and Wong, A. (eds.) (1986) *Language of the Black experience* Blackwell

Trudgill, P. (1975) *Accent, dialect and the school* Edward Arnold

Trudgill, P. (ed.) (1984) *Language in the British Isles* Cambridge University Press

Wakelin, M. F. (1977) *English dialects: An introduction* Athlone Press

Wakelin, M. F. (1985) *English dialects* Shire Publications

Historical variation

Aitchison, J. (1986) *Language change: Progress or decay?* Fontana

Baugh, A. C. and Cable, T. (1978) *History of the English language* Routledge and Kegan Paul

Greenbaum, S. (1984) *The English language today* Pergamon Press

Jenkins, C. (1980) *Language links: The European family of languages* Harrap

Lass, R. (1987) *The shape of English: Structure and history* Dent

Lockwood, W. B. (1975) *Languages of the British Isles past and present* Deutsch

Scragg, D. G. (1975) *History of English spelling* Manchester University Press

Strang, B. M. H. (1974) *History of English* Methuen

Tucker, S. I. (1961) *English examined: Two centuries of comment on the mother-tongue* Cambridge University Press

Appendix 8 *The model in summary form*

See fold-out attached inside back cover.

Printed in the United Kingdom for Her Majesty's Stationery Office Dd 239495 C250 4/88